The Five Rules

Advance Praise for
The 5 Rules

"I first met Steve eight years ago at one of my executive events in Atlanta. That year he became a member of my inner circle, and I coached and mentored him personally over the next year. At dinner during that first event, I challenged him to write a set of 5 rules he could teach and coach from, and he did just that. Those 5 foundational behavior rules he follows, his teams follow, and his family has followed over these last eight years are legacy building at its best. Now to see it come to life in his first book is thrilling to me. As I always say, leadership is influence, and he's used his influence to lead thousands of team members in the grocery companies he's led across the country since then. I know he's sharing several things in this book we teach at the John Maxwell companies, and I'm especially happy he shares a top leadership lesson my father taught me: 'walk slowly through the crowds.' I encourage you to 'walk slowly through the chapters of this book.' Its pages are filled with common sense—everyday leader-

ship lessons that can truly change your world and your own inner circle."

Dr. John C. Maxwell
#1 *New York Times* Best Selling Author,
over 35 million books sold in 50 languages
#1 Leader in business and most influential leadership
expert in the world by *Inc. Magazine*

"The 5 Rules are a simple breakdown for success in a complicated world. Living out these principles in our family has been a game changer! Built on a lifetime of experience, I'm proud to say my dad has created a living legacy for his family—something to pass down for generations. Simple, yet extremely challenging at times, these 5 Rules help me become a better husband, father, son, and friend. Personal growth is a journey—and whether at home or in a professional environment, one can make it 'A Brighter Day' for those around you by living out these 5 Rules. I challenge you to take an introspective look as you make the 5 Rules part of your daily life!"

Jared Stephen Black
Vice President, Solution Sales,
TRUNO Retail Technology Solutions

"When my dad introduced his 5 Rules to me halfway through my career, I loved the concept for all the intangibles that we seek in our business; more importantly, it gave a measurement that we could lead, coach, and guide from. I have implemented these rules to some of the most successful teams, and not only have they impacted our business to help achieve results not seen before, but yielded the highest teammate satisfaction along with growth that was exceptionally high for all who were involved. The rules, as successful as they have been for my business, are as successfully transferable to your personal life, in two words that describe it perfectly … GAME CHANGER!"

Travis Douglas Black

General Manager, Shottenkirk Chevrolet Waukee, IA

"Clear, concise, and compelling! In The 5 Rules, Steve Black adeptly describes and illustrates key components of a healthy culture. Utilizing these insights, any organization can effectively shape team dynamics that will produce an environment in which people can flourish, elevating both engagement and productivity."

Dr. Randy Ross

Best-Selling Author, Founder & CEO of Remarkable!

"Let The 5 Rules Culture Improvement stats speak for themselves. We've had them in place for over four years now. Overall growth on State Assessment Index went up 3 basis points, formal write-ups went down 70%, and out-of-school suspension rates were cut by over 50%. 70% of students are now involved in extracurricular activities. The football team went from a 2–4 record to a 5–2 record and has been undefeated the last three years and won the district championship. The team is united like never before using the 5 Rules as a foundation for behaviors."

Jason Corbin
Houma Junior High Principal, Houma, LA

"One of the most fundamental elements of leadership is establishing a culture of success within an organization, which can only be accomplished once team members fully understand their leader's performance and behavioral expectations. In his book, The 5 Rules, Steve Black provides leaders with a practical framework to assist them in setting and communicating those expectations. As a bit of 'lagniappe,' he also gives some excellent leadership advice: 'always, always, always assume the mic is hot.'"

Ray Peters, MS, SPHR, SHRM-SCP
Instructor of Leadership and Former MBA Director,
Nicholls State University, Thibodaux, LA

"I found The 5 Rules by Steve Black to be a great read. It's a highly distilled lifetime of practical life lessons that will help you become the leader that teammates want to work for and follow, the nurturing parent and spouse your family needs, and the businessperson others wish to do business with, all in a quick read. He is the kind of guy that you can trust because he is clear, consistent, and rock-solid in his convictions. In his book, you'll read the heartwarming and authentic stories of his life's interactions and experiences with family, friends, coworkers, bosses, and teammates, which he cleverly transformed into an easily transferrable and repeatable 'five rules' approach toward setting and fulfilling mutual expectations. These lessons and principles can and will positively impact leaders and future leaders at any stage and, simply put, help you become a better person. I highly recommend the book!"

David Smith
President & CEO, Associated Wholesale Grocers

"Great and practical advice for any part of your life. The section on being positive is spot on. A negative person will never lead or create a team."

Mike Scholtman
CFO Kroger, retired

"Steve Black's 5 Rules are essential to creating the right culture in the workplace and at home, something that is so important today. His delivery and storytelling are easy to relate to, truly impactful, and should be mandatory reading for leaders everywhere!"

Greg Ferrara
President & CEO, National Grocers Association

"I've known Steve for over 15 years as a colleague, a customer, a mentor, and most importantly, as a friend. Over the years, I've watched Steve lead and inspire so many people with a true passion for their success. Steve builds relationships always to help others see strengths they may not have seen in themselves. In Steve's book, The 5 Rules, you will see a simple approach to improving your leadership and relationship skills at work, at home, and in your community. Steve understands that we are time starved and leadership hungry, and he shares stories and tips in a way that keeps you motivated to keep reading. The 5 Rules can and will make a difference when you put them to work. Enjoy the journey . . . "

Jeff Pedersen
President & CEO,Retailer Owned
Food Distributors and Associates, "ROFDA"

"Steve Black brings more than 45 years of leadership experience to life in this very readable guide to culture transformation. His detailed recollections of influencers throughout his journey coupled with compelling examples of applying the 5 Rules make this book very difficult to put down. This 'how to' narrative is a must-read for anyone in a leadership role whether in their family, department, or corporation. I love this book for its easily applicable and valuable lessons, and I've already used many of them. This will be continuous reading for my personal growth trajectory and a 'company manual' for any organization I lead."

Stephanie Reid
President & Publisher, Shelby Publishing, Inc.

"While most leadership books only offer lessons in your professional and business career, these are family and life skills that are sure to raise your leadership lid in every aspect of daily life. The 5 Rules should be on your must-read list."

Joe Boudreaux
CEO, The Boudreaux Group, Keller Williams Realty

"Steve Black's framework for the 5 Rules is disarmingly simple and easy to understand, yet applicable across all professional and personal aspects of your life."

Harold Callais II
Managing Partner, Callais Capital

"Everyone who reads this book can't help but self-reflect on how they live their life and walk away committed to be a better version of themselves. Steve Black, through the life lessons and experiences he humbly and openly shares, brings to life just how simply we can bring out the best in ourselves and others through his 5 Rules. Nothing beats learning good coaching and leadership skills from a truly great and respected coach and leader."

Scott Welman,
Principal, The Food Partners, LLC

"The 5 Rules are so simple, yet so relevant to our world today that my team and I live by them in our day-to-day activities. Surprisingly, my family also adopted them in our daily lives!"

J.J. Cantrell
President, UNFI

"Steve Black's 5 Rules will illuminate the path for how to live with excellence, lead teams with integrity, and build a rock-solid foundation based on healthy relationships and a thriving team culture. A leader who knows the way, goes the way, and shows the way, Steve will help you bring joy and brighter days back to your life's work!"

Traci Morrow
Relationship Expert for Maxwell Leadership,
Co-Host of Maxwell Leadership Podcast, and
Amazon Best Selling Author of *Real-Life Marriage*

"This book is very easy reading and relatable. The lessons taught through the eyes of Steve's experience whether through his family, mentors or work experience make it real. I took notes the entire time I was reading the script and as I'm sure was the plan on the purpose of the book, challenging the reader to think, apply and learn! The 5 Rules are the foundation of building relationships and a healthy culture. Our company is built on these foundations! We launched the 5 Rules while I was in the New Orleans market and it's still going strong today by uniting the teams and giving everyone a common language of expected behaviors to keep the culture rock solid."

Susanne Hall
SVP & Chief Commercial Officer, Coke United

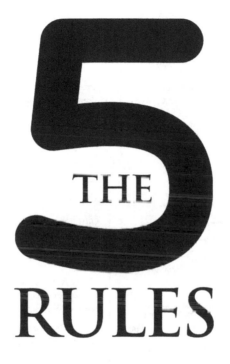

THE 5 RULES

Transform Your Culture for Yourself, Your Team, and Your Family

STEPHEN D. BLACK

NEW YORK

LONDON • NASHVILLE • MELBOURNE • VANCOUVER

The Five Rules

Transform Your Culture for Yourself, Your Team and Your Family

Published in New York, New York, by Morgan James Publishing. Morgan James is a trademark of Morgan James, LLC. www.MorganJamesPublishing.com

Proudly distributed by Publishers Group West®

A FREE ebook edition is available for you or a friend with the purchase of this print book.

CLEARLY SIGN YOUR NAME ABOVE

Instructions to claim your free ebook edition:
1. Visit MorganJamesBOGO.com
2. Sign your name CLEARLY in the space above
3. Complete the form and submit a photo of this entire page
4. You or your friend can download the ebook to your preferred device

ISBN 9781636982014 paperback
ISBN 9781636982021 ebook
Library of Congress Control Number:
2023936307

Cover & Interior Design by:
Christopher Kirk
www.GFSstudio.com

Cover Concept by:
Best Seller Publishing

Morgan James is a proud partner of Habitat for Humanity Peninsula and Greater Williamsburg. Partners in building since 2006.

Get involved today! Visit: www.morgan-james-publishing.com/giving-back

DEDICATION

I want to dedicate this book to my 4th-grade sweetheart and wife of 46 years, Melanie Janell Roll Black. Thank you for helping me along this journey, and I look forward to many more years of enjoying this ride with you.

My oldest son, Jared, who has now begun to add second-generation leadership lessons on our website and is raising his two sons, Dax and Brody, with his wife, Beth, in Texas.

My son Travis, who has also added his own leadership lessons on the website and is raising his four daughters, Avayah, Adalynne, Amelia, and Anabella with his wife, Sarah, in Iowa.

My daughter, Taylor Janell Black, who you'll read about in this book. She has completed our family in a way nobody else could have.

As you'll read through this book, family is everything. These are the most important relationships you have on this earth. Keep them fun and healthy!

TABLE OF CONTENTS

ACKNOWLEDGMENTS

I'd like to thank the team at Best Seller Publishing for all the help and guidance in helping bring this dream to life. Rob Kosberg and Bob Harpole have been great to work with from the beginning to where we are today. Bob was very instrumental with every chapter submission with his insight and advice about putting the best possible content together which resulted in a smooth flow for the entire book. They also have a great support team to help along the way.

I'd also like to thank David Hancock, Founder & Publisher of Morgan James Publishing for the continued help and guidance to get this book into brick-and-mortar stores around the globe. He and his team have a clear vision of best practices and they have built great relationships in the business over the last twenty years.

It's been great to meet new people along life's journey that add value to your own journey, and I've found that in these two companies!

INTRODUCTION

Wouldn't you love it if everyone in your life followed the same set of rules?

In *The 5 Rules: Transform Your Culture for Yourself, Your Team and Your Family*, I set out a simple set of **expected behaviors**, behaviors you can expect from yourself and others. Once you truly understand the depth and simplicity of them, you can use them in your daily life and in all your relationships, both professional and personal.

The 5 Rules have served me well now for over two decades. These rules are very alive and well in my family, my sons' families, and those of my grandchildren. They have also leveled the playing field in my work life. I have decades of testimony from people who have implemented these rules in their businesses and personal lives, and they've truly made a difference. I hope they will do the same for you.

A former business associate of mine, Mr. Tony Stafford, who worked for Valu Merchandisers, a subsidiary of Associated Wholesale Grocers out of Kansas City, Kansas, first introduced me to his three rules. He allowed me to borrow a couple of them and expand them to my five rules.

I have discovered these rules over my 45-year career in the retail grocery space, where I went from managing stores in one state to managing stores in 14 states. My humble beginnings were as a produce manager in Weatherford, Oklahoma, managing just a few people. Recently, I retired from my role as President and Chief Operating Officer for a Gulf Coast grocery chain operating in three states. In this role, I have had the privilege to serve over seven thousand team members out of our headquarters in Thibodaux, Louisiana. During my work life, I was fortunate enough to lead many business departments, including operations, marketing, information technology, and sales and purchasing. I have discovered that the best part of the 5 Rules is that they are effective in all locations and in all departments. I've always said, "We are in the people business; we just happen to sell groceries!"

> "We are in the people business; we just happen to sell groceries!"

"Expected Behaviors," which are the foundation of each rule, are a challenge in our world today. People come from different backgrounds and have different upbringings and personal histories, and their worldviews vary greatly. These rules have a way of bringing everyone together on one page. They allow us to hold each other accountable. When anyone breaks one of the five rules, we can have a calm conversation and discuss our level of commitment to the rules. They also give us a path to move forward, unified and resolved that our lives will be better as we follow them.

The word "culture" is a common term. I think it is overused in almost all circles, including businesses, churches, schools, and homes. But I wonder if most people could explain in a nutshell what culture is. Here's what I think culture is: it's the emotion you feel about a place you have to go to or a person you have to meet.

1. I have to go to work … ugh
2. I have to go see the boss … ugh
3. I have to go to church … ugh
4. I have to go to school … ugh
5. I have to go home … ugh

Is this the way you feel? How many "ughs" do you have in your life?

"Ughs" are a sign of a bad culture, and I believe that what makes a culture bad is having different sets of rules for all the different groups of people who are part of that culture. If there is a different set of rules (expected behaviors) that the executive team goes by, a different set of rules that the corporate office team goes by, and another set of rules that the store teams go by, the core culture of the company is confused. It becomes difficult to hold anyone accountable for their behaviors. If we are on the same team, we should play by the same rules!

As this book will reveal, if the 5 Rules are alive in all your circles, you can turn your "ughs" into something much more positive.

1. I can't wait to go to work today!
2. I'm meeting with the best boss I've ever had this afternoon!
3. I'm so looking forward to the church services this Sunday!
4. I can't wait to see my teachers and classmates at school tomorrow!
5. I just love going home to my bride and my kiddos!

When I was developing the website for the 5 Rules, I had to decide on a domain name. Our first choice was abrighterday.com because I've always thought that if we embrace and follow the 5 Rules, we can all have brighter days. But that domain was unavailable. However, abrighterday.life *was* available. A lightbulb went off! Imagine both a brighter day and a brighter life!!! And so our new home online began.

I knew then that these 5 Rules were bigger than me, and I just had to launch that website and pursue this passion to help make brighter days in the lives of people around the world. My hope is that you'll embrace, trust, and implement these 5 Rules. Embed them into your culture. And if you do, I guarantee you that you'll have brighter days. Just like the image on the cover!

Now, let's get right into Rule 1—Do Your Job! Can you imagine living in a world where everyone just did their job?

RULE 1: DO YOUR JOB

This book is a rock solid guide of expectations that will transform the culture of your team, your family, and yourself. The first rule: Do Your Job. At first glance, this rule seems so simple. It's easy to skim over it and think, "Well, of course, the first rule should be to do your job." Not so fast! It is so important that you know what your job is. What I have found over the years is that a lot of people think they know what their job is, but they really don't. Either they haven't been trained in what their job is, or they've been trained by the wrong person.

As a team leader, this means that you need to 1) Make sure your team members understand what exactly their job is; 2) Make sure that each team member is qualified to do their actual job; and 3) Do YOUR Job to make the whole team better.

Drive-Thru Communication

From a leadership standpoint, you might think somebody understands their job. I suggest trying "Drive-thru Communication" to make sure this is the case. When you pull up to a drive-thru window at a fast food restaurant, the first thing you do is give your order into the speaker. Then, the cashier repeats it back to you. That's when you give them a job and they confirm what their job is. Sometimes as leaders, we need to do this same thing. Have your team members describe their job to you in their own words. You can say either, "Yes, that's right," or "No, that's close, but it's not quite spot on. Let me add a few more pieces to that description." Then they'll understand *exactly* what their job is.

When Someone You Lead Isn't Doing Their Job

If you find that someone you are leading is not following Rule 1, you have a few options. As Jim Collins shares in his book *Good to Great*, "The first option is the right people on the bus. Second is the wrong people off the bus. But third is the right people in the right seats."[1] Asking someone to get off the bus doesn't mean they are a bad person; it just means that they aren't qualified to do the job they have been asked to do. My first option is

---

1   Jim Collins. *Good to Great: Why Some Companies Make the Leap … and Others Don't* (New York: HarperBusiness, 2001).

always to keep them on the bus. And if that doesn't work out, I will ask them to leave the bus and find another bus that better fits their skill set.

DIFFERENT WAYS TO READ THE RULE

There are three different ways that you can read Rule 1. You can emphasize each of the three words and it gives a different meaning to the rule.

- DO Your Job
- Do YOUR Job
- Do Your JOB

I think the "Do YOUR Job" is the most used variation of the rule. But each of them has its own unique application.

One of the best examples of this came from Tyler Price, a former colleague of mine at United Supermarkets of Oklahoma. He often described the role of the guy you always see on the football game sidelines and he has one job to do. You've all seen him. His job is to keep the football clean and dry. And my goodness, the passion and enthusiasm that he tackles this job with is remarkable. He sprints along the sidelines closest to the ball, gets it between plays, dries it off, and stands alert—ready for the next play. That's all he has to worry about. He doesn't have to take tickets, sell concessions, or clean up after everyone leaves. He just has to keep the ball clean and dry.

DO YOUR JOB

Making the Whole Team Better

In retail stores, which are "for-profit" businesses, we pay people to do their jobs, and we simply ask them to hold up their end of the agreement. We also challenge our team members to be IMPACT players: players who change the outcome of the game. Not once, but every time. When you're an impact player, you make the whole team better.

That is what Magic Johnson learned early in his basketball career. He was very successful as an individual player but quickly realized that his job was to actually make the whole team better. And he did. Every game. Every season. Every level.

On the home front, I need to do my job there as well. I often joke that it's my job to pay the mortgage and take out the trash! But seriously, it's my job to HAVE a job, to make sure my family is taken care of and feels secure. When our children were growing up, it was also my job to coach, train, and encourage them to be productive adults. It's my job at home to be the same kind of leader there as I am at work. Obviously not the same way, but to make sure the outcome is the same. And that's simply to help everyone feel safe and secure. It's imperative that I have a consistent mood and am happy, present, and fun to be around.

Five Life Lessons on
Doing Your Job—Only Better!

Life Lesson One: It doesn't matter what you can do, it matters what you *do*!

This line was born while I was coaching my youngest son, Travis, in city league baseball in Altus, Oklahoma, when he was twelve years old.

I started coaching him in city league basketball when he was only five years old. Earlier that year, his coach had the team of five-year-olds trying to run plays, instead of just teaching them the basic fundamentals of basketball and it was driving me crazy. As I sat in the stands griping about it to Melanie, my wife, she just looked straight ahead and without missing a beat said to me, "Well, Steve, why don't you coach his team?" That comment left me feeling somewhat like Michael Oher's coach after a coaching lesson from Mrs. Tuohy in the movie *The Blind Side*.

What my wife said made sense to me. She taught me this simple lesson—"Don't gripe, DO!" So I started my coaching career. And during all those early years, I just taught basic fundamentals, passing, dribbling, shooting, rebounding, and NOT walking. Little did I know that this time period in my life would actually come in pretty handy when I began to lead bigger teams in my role at work.

Before you get too detailed with complicated business plans, make sure the team knows the basic fundamentals of retail. For example, truly know how to calculate gross margin!

My son Travis has a God-given gift for athletics. He's great at basketball and baseball. He's a real natural talent where success comes easy. Throughout all the years of his city league career, our teams were normally undefeated and won the championships. We were always accused of having the "stacked" team, although we put together teams using all the same rules as everyone else. It was fair, but having someone like Travis on an already great team made it feel like someone had broken the rules. We see this in sports and in business. It's the natural tendency to play just hard enough to win. Or in business, to just stay a little bit ahead of your closest competitor.

If you're going to be the best, you have to be YOUR best every time out. You have to be YOUR best when nobody is looking. Whether it's an actual game or in business if you're going into a new market. You have to give it all you have. In sports, if you want to win more than you lose, you don't have to just play harder than the competition, you also have to overcome bad calls (i.e., circumstances beyond your control). In business, I believe that if you are truly running the best store possible, you should be able to pick it up and place it in any city in the country and still have a successful store.

Back to coaching Travis …

When you have a player who can score in basketball anytime he wants to, hit a home run at any given time, or pitch a no-hitter, you really have to try to keep him focused on humility and keeping himself in check. It was in the fifth grade that I coached one of his city league baseball teams and we knew this would be our last year there. We didn't do very well that summer and it was primarily due to the arrogance of the whole team. After all, we'd won the championship every year for the last several years. Even with all the talent that they all possessed, we were getting killed in one particular game and in one of our timeouts, as the team was gathered around me, these words came out of my mouth:

"Every one of you is the best at the position you play. Nobody on the other team is better than any one of you."

It doesn't matter what you can do, it matters what you *do*!

Going into the fifth inning, we were down by five runs. In the bottom of the fifth, Travis caught fire with his bat. He hit a solo home run, a two-run homer, and a grand slam (that's seven RBIs—runs he batted in). He also pitched the final innings of the game with multiple strikeouts. Going into the fifth inning, our team got a fire in their bellies that made them rise up and prove that it is *what you do* that matters!

As you might guess, we won the game!

Life Lesson Two: The Three Great Separators

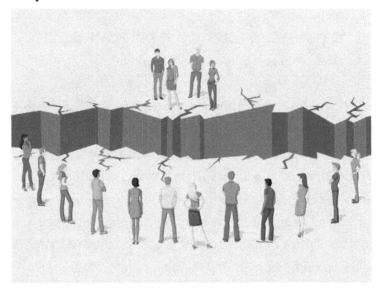

Over my 45-year career in the grocery retail space, I've experienced what I call the three great separators: **technology**, **leadership**, and **attitude**. These are the elements of change or critical personality traits that truly separate you from the crowd and will almost guarantee success.

It's really about those who have a *growth mindset*, versus a *fixed mindset*. If you have a growth mindset, there is no limit to what you can achieve if you are willing to put in the hard work to learn something new, to get out of your comfort zone and grow in your knowledge and career. If you have a fixed mindset, you believe that you are destined to only go so high in your career and you can't really do anything about it. You're not very willing to learn new things or improve on your skill sets or personality. You are kind of a "go-with-the-flow" person.

As we explore each of the three great separators, you'll see how a *growth mindset* versus a *fixed mindset* is what sets people apart.

The First Separator: Technology

The first great separator I noticed began in the 1980s. But first you must understand that I grew up in western Oklahoma and graduated from high school in 1977. When I graduated high school, we didn't have any computers in the building. For typing class, we had IBM electric typewriters. Yep, that's it. Oh, and electric adding machines.

I worked for United Supermarkets of Oklahoma right out of high school and in 1986, while I was a store director in Weatherford, the company decided to put in scanning systems. I was tapped to drive the new initiative but had zero computer training, and I had zero programming knowledge. But I was hungry to learn. Being a current store director as well, I didn't have a lot of time to learn the details of my new task. I attended two days of training on the scanning systems and returned ready to go! We had twenty-seven stores, and our plan was to convert about five stores a year until we got them all upgraded. With great team effort, our plan was successful.

Fast-forward to 2014—I was living in Phoenix, Arizona, and onboard with Sunflower Farmers Market as VP of IT and Marketing. After a buyout by Sprouts Farmers Market, I became the Chief Information Officer and Chief Marketing Officer of Sprouts. Little did I know just how much the experience at United would pay future dividends. We went from a 37-store chain to now a 154-store chain, and I was in charge of leading the IT team and the marketing team. If I hadn't ever taken that step to get on board with the information technology train, I'm not sure where I'd be today. Instead of doors closing, they were opening.

What I discovered was that if you truly knew how to interpret and program data and learn systems, you could mine that data and put together the information you needed to excel in your role. If you couldn't, the company had to hire an administrative person to do those tasks for you. And today, that model just simply doesn't work.

The separation I saw during those years was that those in my peer group who didn't embrace technology, or care to learn about it, arc basically at the same level they were at twenty-five years before. Very few ever advanced higher in their careers.

When I'm interviewing someone for a leadership role, one of the top questions I ask is, "Can you tell me your skill level in technology?" I specifically ask about their knowledge of the latest Office application, or other applications that are business-related. With the right answer, the candidate moves on through the interview process; with the wrong answer, the interview is basically over.

The Second Separator: Leadership

The second great separator is leadership. Not as a position of management, but the quality of being truly interested in leadership growth. John Maxwell is known for his statement about leadership: that it is critical for having a long career in higher roles.

A lot of people believe that reading books and always growing in your leadership style is a bunch of

Everything rises and falls on leadership.

John Maxwell

kumbaya stuff. And that mindset is exactly why some people are *separated from the crowd*. It doesn't matter what role you have; unless you are a one-person operation, there is no way you can do everything. The quicker you learn that you need people to be successful, and the quicker you learn how to inspire them to greatness, the quicker success will come your and your company's way. And by the way, you don't just need people, you need the RIGHT people. If you have the wrong people on the bus, your leadership direction will fall on deaf ears. Don't waste your time on people who care nothing about leadership.

You have to be hungry, your team has to be hungry, and you have to lock arms and intentionally grow your leadership skills together. A *one team* mindset is critical. When you come in with a leadership focus, what happens over time is that those who don't embrace leadership will stand out among the group so clearly that you'll be forced to allow them to move on. It's their choice.

I've experienced those who wrap their arms around leadership growth so strongly that you have no choice but to continue to promote them and give them more and more responsibilities. They will figure it out and that's the type of team member you want in the foxhole fighting with you.

The Third Separator: An Insatiable Positive Attitude

The third great separator is an insatiable positive attitude. The retail grocery business will chew you up and spit you out if you don't have a positive attitude. I've known people who have spent their entire careers letting the pressures of dealing with cranky customers, cranky team members, cranky vendors, and cranky bosses drive them into the most negative attitude you can imagine.

I like to think of it like the story I heard several years ago about the farmer who had a donkey that fell into an empty well.

After observing the donkey down in the well, the farmer made the decision that he had no way to get him out, so he decided to put him out of his misery and just

bury him. He gathered up some of his friends and they began to put shovels of dirt down in the well. As each shovel of dirt fell onto the donkey's back, to their amazement, he just shook it off. After enough shovels of dirt had been shaken off, he took a step up. After three hours of repeating this, the donkey just stepped out of the well and went on his way. I've worked with some people who, no matter what comes their way, they figure out "how to shake it off and step up higher."

If you've worked with anyone with an insatiable negative attitude, you know they suck the life out of everyone around them and the rooms they are in. They've got to go. When I think of people over my 45-year career that I've had to open the bus door for and let off, they normally possess the negative element of all three of these great separators. If you're interested in growing your career and getting the most out of what this ol' life has to offer, I'd recommend you focus on these top three separators.

To me, everything else is coachable!

My best skill was that I was coachable. I was a sponge and aggresive to learn.

Michael Jordan

Life Lesson Three: The Five Traits of a Good Boss

Most of my writings have been about the positive influences of people in my life over the years. One of my bosses early in my career told me that I'd learn more from my bad bosses than the good ones. I thought it was a good one-liner at the time; however, little did I know just how true that would be over the next 45 years.

The gist of that comment was that the good bosses are normally so smooth and good at what they do, it's easy to learn from them. You emulate them without realizing you are learning. But the bad bosses' behaviors and their detrimental traits are so seared into your mind that you truly do learn more from them; you learn what NOT to do.

Obviously, I'll leave out names, but bad bosses have taught me a lot over the years. Below I've listed the traits that every good boss should have.

Bad Bosses provide powerful lessons.

Trait One: Be Consistent

By far, the single most important thing I've learned from bad bosses is to be consistent. For goodness' sake, be the same person today that you were yesterday.

Nothing drives your team crazier than inconsistency. One day you're up, the next day you're down. One day you want something done this way, the very next day you want it done differently. As John Maxwell says, "When you do that, you put your team in a tailspin."

If you know me at all, you know that all my business lessons work at home. If you're a parent, trust me, this is a big one at home. You need to be consistent. If you reprimand your kids for not cleaning their room or doing their homework, do it every time or not at all. (Another parenting tip: "When milk is running off the table, nobody needs a speech, just a towel." Give your kids a break on the speeches; they didn't do it on purpose! *I learned this one the hard way*.)

Trait Two: Have True Compassion

The second most important quality that you won't see in bad bosses is true compassion. They are typically selfish and are diminishers. Diminishers have these five negative qualities, as discussed in the book *Multipliers* by Liz Wiseman.[2]

1. The Empire Builder (Hoards resources and underutilizes talent)
2. The Tyrant (Creates a tense environment that suppresses people's thinking and capability)

---

2   Liz Wiseman and Greg McKeown. *Multipliers: How the Best Leaders Make Everyone Smarter* (New York: HarperBusiness, 2010).

3. The Know-It-All (Gives directives that showcase how much they know)
4. The Decision Maker (Makes centralized, abrupt decisions that confuse the organization)
5. The Micro Manager (Drives results through their personal involvement)

Do any former bosses come to mind after reading these?

Most of us have seen the quote from Maya Angelou below and it's one of my favorites:

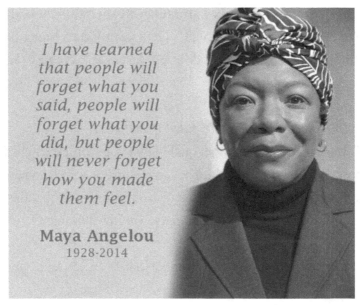

I have learned that people will forget what you said, people will forget what you did, but people will never forget how you made them feel.

Maya Angelou
1928-2014

Again, whether a boss or a parent, this quote has the inspiration to change you. Most of the time you can't remember what a "bad boss" said, but, man, you do remember how they made you feel. Emotions are truly at the heart of whether you enjoyed or didn't enjoy working for them. Sadly, you probably won't realize how much oppression you are under working for a bad boss until you're no longer working for them. And we've all heard this before: "People don't quit companies, they quit bosses!"

I've shared with my team on more than one occasion that, as a boss, you WILL be the topic of your direct reports' dinner table conversation at some point and most likely will be the subject of one of the first few questions they'll be asked when they get home. "Give them something good to say," is my constant challenge to them, and myself.

Trait Three: Teach People How to Do Their Job Better

The third most important quality is the ability to teach people how to do their job. Bad bosses don't teach you anything about how to do your job better. It's because they probably don't know themselves. In my early years in the grocery retail space, my work life was so challenging because the guy making the main decisions didn't have a clue about the details of what made the business successful or not. That's why in most organizations, the better leaders have come up through the ranks and held enough different positions that they truly do know the key details of how to run the business.

Trait Four: Have a Backbone

The fourth most important quality that you won't see in a bad boss is a backbone. I'm sure many of you have experienced a boss who was horrible at making a decision and sticking to it. You always wanted to be the last one to speak to them about something because whoever got the last conversation, won the verdict. They were all big and bad and acted like they had a backbone until someone else on the team talked to them; then they'd cave over the smallest detail and reverse the previous decision. If you truly want the respect of your team, gather information, determine the potential short- and long-term outcome, and then make your final decision and stick to it!

Trait Five: Give Credit Where Credit Is Due

The fifth most important quality that you won't see in a bad boss is giving credit where credit is due, or taking blame. If you watch any professional sporting event, you'll see the coaches get interviewed at the end of the game. You'll never hear a coach stand there and tell you the team won because of the coaching. They will ALWAYS give credit to the other team and insist that their team won because of the players and other coaches. In a loss, a great coach will take 100 percent of the blame. This is called class. Praise in public, criticize in private.

There you have it: the five key traits of a good boss.

These five traits are not something that you are born knowing. They are learned behaviors and can be adopted and embraced. Some people may have to work harder to be able to exhibit these traits, but they are achievable for everyone. Even those folks who are currently bad bosses.

Life Lesson Four: Driver or Passenger?

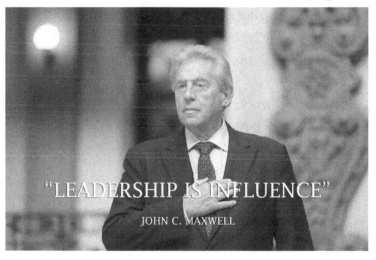

"LEADERSHIP IS INFLUENCE"

JOHN C. MAXWELL

John Maxwell's mantra may sound simple, but sometimes it can be hard to understand. He believes in it so much, a sign with these three simple words hangs in the lobby of his offices: Leadership is Influence. My interpretation of those three words is also simple. Everyone has influence, some negative and some positive. If you're a leader, the influence MUST be positive, and you MUST be a driver! Every team needs passengers, but the leader of a store or support office department can't be a passenger.

Here are the key components of being a driver:

- Always looking to improve your area of responsibility
- Always looking to improve yourself
- Knowing how to ask the right questions
- Knowing how to get the right answers
- Having a strong sense of urgency

If you are in a leadership role and are a passenger, here is what you look like:

- Just making the donuts
- Never reading or watching anything on improving yourself
- Not asking the right questions
- Not having any answers
- Never driving any initiatives

With this I say: You're Either a Driver or You're Not!

Sadly, some people in leadership positions aren't only *not* driving the bus; they aren't even on it!

SOME PEOPLE MAKE THINGS HAPPEN, SOME WATCH THINGS HAPPEN, WHILE OTHERS WONDER WHAT HAS HAPPENED.

So, you might ask, "How do I become a driver?" One of my coaching lessons to store directors is that anyone should be able to walk into your store and, from a distance, immediately spot that you are the person in charge. Here are three ways to achieve this:

1. Look like a store director, by
   - The way you dress
   - The way you make eye contact
   - The way you walk, with a sense of urgency
2. Act like you're in charge, by
   - The way you're engaged with the team
   - The way you're engaged with vendors
   - The way you're engaged with customers
3. Have charisma and presence, by
   - Having an outgoing personality
   - Listening intently — with your ears and your eyes
   - Speaking confidently

If you want to be a driver, you MUST have Charisma and Presence.

Who wants to follow someone with no charisma or no presence? And you can rest assured that the level of energy, charisma, and presence of your team will be below where yours is. So set the bar high! If you look back over the last week, and you did nothing extra that wouldn't have been done except for the fact that you drove it—you're a passenger.

Be a driver, or wind up a passenger!

Here are some of my coaching lessons to corporate home office leadership members. It is important to have these qualities:

1. You look like a professional, by
   - The way you dress
   - The way you talk
   - The way you treat everyone in the office
2. You're engaging and organized, and
   - Friendly to all departments, not just yours
   - You keep a clean and organized office
   - You're always willing to help others
3. You know how to conduct a meeting, by
   - Publishing an agenda
   - Starting and ending on time
   - Sending out recaps of timelines and deliverable action items

Life Lesson Five: Do Your Job—Raise Your Hand!

It's not a crime to have a problem, but it is a crime to have a problem and not raise your hand!

So many people think that "Do Your Job" means you must do it all by yourself and that if you can't do it, then you've failed. Nothing could be further from the truth. Raising your hand to let someone know you need help is truly Doing Your Job! If you think about it, part of doing your job is making sure the job gets done! In most organizations, there are layers of support that can be brought in or just moved around inside the store to help get you out of a ditch.

I can't tell you how many times I've been on store visits and run into a critical issue that could have been solved in a very short time if I'd just known about it or, quite frankly, if anyone had known about it. Again, most companies have local, regional, and national resources that are available on short notice. With today's worldwide supply chain and employment challenges at an all-time high, very few days go as planned. There are late trucks, product outages, and daily call-ins and no-shows.

Today, more than ever, a leader better be an all-star "audible caller." Just like a quarterback in a football game who walks up to the line with the pre-called play in mind—once they see a different configuration of the defense, they must call a different play. Be confident and flexible when snap decisions need to be made.

CHAPTER SUMMARY

There you have it—*behavior expectations* on Rule #1!

My goal is that each of the lessons in this chapter will stir something inside of you, and you'll accept the challenge of making this behavior core to who you are.

It's also critical, as you begin to coach this rule to those around you, that they see that you live this rule, every day, in every situation, and in every role you have. Without that, you will not have the influence you need to have.

Before people will follow you, they must trust you.

> Trust is built when your walk matches your talk.

Bring It to Life

1. Write down your top three roles—in Personal life and Work life.
2. Give yourself a grade on how you think you're doing in each area.

3. Write down two things that you can do better, starting today.
4. Ask someone to hold you accountable.

Reader's Bonus

Since you're reading this book, I know you have an interest in improving your culture. Based on Rule 1, I would like to give you a reader's bonus. I will do this with each rule. I hope you find this as helpful as I have.

You can find all of the bonuses here: abrighterday. life/bonuses

Rule 2: Be Kind

Being kind doesn't mean being a pushover. It doesn't mean that you don't hold people accountable to do their job. It means you don't demean people with your tone, word choices, or actions. One of my favorite sayings: I can tell you everything I need to know about you by the way that you treat the person who can do nothing for you.

> I can tell you everything I need to know about you by the way that you treat the person who can do nothing for you.

It's easy to be nice to your boss, the principal of the school, the president of the bank, or your best friend. It's not so easy to be nice to slow drivers, incompetent cashiers, demanding customers, or a co-worker who is difficult to work with or be around. Being kind isn't always easy. But it's always right.

Being kind isn't always easy. But it's always right

As a boss, being kind is especially important to your success as a leader and the success of your team. From a leadership standpoint, *you* are the example for your team, and this is where the attempt to get people to follow the 5 Rules will fail if you're not kind (to everyone). Your team will always follow what you DO—more than what you SAY.

Over my career, I've had to terminate employment for some people, not because they were incompetent at their job but because they simply couldn't be kind. They weren't kind to our customers (I'll get to the importance of this at the end of the chapter) and they were unkind to our other team members. I often remind my teams that all our paychecks come out of the same bank account, that we all have the same logo on our shirts, and that we should all act like we are on the same team. And we certainly should never shoot our own wounded. Be kind because you never really know what someone is going through. A struggling team member might just need a little extra grace as they deal with something deep or very personal.

While stressing its importance, I must admit this rule presents one of my greatest personal challenges. Not all the time but certainly some of the time. The key for me to follow this rule is just consistency. The secret is to not let moments or situations derail me from my intent to always be kind. In the fast-paced world that we live in, sometimes I let being busy give me a pass on being kind. However, I should never be too busy to be kind.

Being kind at home after the end of a long hard workday is also a challenge. Home is our safe haven, and if we're not careful, our family takes the brunt of our "bad day." I'll cover that a little more under Rule 4, No Drama, but let me give you a quick takeaway. *After reading Rule 4, you'll have a practical way to leave your drama on a towel!*

During our discussion on Rule 2, I will discuss kindness itself and also introduce other elements that tie directly or indirectly to being kind, like being coachable. These two qualities are connected as I believe that if you're kind, you're coachable, and if you're coachable, you will be a kind person. I'm going to be sharing about my Uncle Charles Seigrist, *my kindness mentor*, who is one of the greatest examples I know of showing kindness and coachability in the way he lives. I will also share how giving your blessings (encouragement) to others in order to build them up is one of the greatest ways to show kindness to them.

So, let's take a look at five life lessons on being kind. If you follow these, you will be a better leader, a better person, and a better partner. Some of them are easy. Some of them are more challenging. But if you commit to being a kinder person, it will pay dividends throughout all aspects of your life. Let's get started!

Five Life Lessons on Being Kind—Only Better!

Life Lesson One: Above All Else …

The question to start with is a simple one: What do you believe ABOVE ALL ELSE?

King Solomon, the second child of David and Bathsheba from the Old Testament, is quoted for many things. He was the King of Israel from 970 to 931 BC. He was very wealthy and was considered by many to be the wisest man who ever lived. In Chapter 4 of Proverbs, King Solomon gives advice to one of his sons. He says, "Above all else …"

I want to stop here.

Think about that for a minute. The wisest and richest man to live in those times is about to tell you something that should be placed above everything. You'd want to listen carefully. I can visualize everyone in his audience looking up, paying careful attention to the words that were about to come out of his mouth.

Are you ready?

He said, "Above all else … guard your heart!"

Guard. Your. Heart.

To me, that means we must be very careful what we allow ourselves to be in love with—what we allow ourselves to be *emotionally* caught by. Everyone who has much experience in life has witnessed people making

Above all else,
guard your heart,
for everything
you do flows
from it.

Provebs 4:23

some horrible decisions and, you'd have to agree, it was most likely because something took over their emotions that really wasn't good for them or their relationships.

In 2014, I attended my first Exchange Conference with Dr. John Maxwell. If you know me at all, you know that I highly respect John, his life, and his legacy. Today, to me, John would be a modern-day King Solomon. He is very wise and very wealthy. At the end of the conference, we had the opportunity to ask him anything we wanted. I stood up and asked John, in the vein of the story of King Solomon and this teaching, how he would finish this statement: Above all else …

He said, "Wow, that's a great question!"

After a few moments of thinking about this, he replied, "Above all else, be true to yourself," and went on to say that most people are so busy trying to please everyone around them, they don't remain true to their convictions and their own self. Many people would probably say something along these same lines as well.

So, I now ask you: How would you finish the statement, "Above all else …"?

Think about it like this: In the next minute, you're going to die. Your family is at your bedside. You've said the last "I love you" and "I will miss you." But you know you have to leave them something that they can carry for the rest of their lives. Something that will give them courage, wisdom, and strength anytime they think about it and those final moments you spent together. What would you say with your last breath?

Here is my answer. Above all else, "Be kind and coachable!"

Being kind and coachable means

- You're not arrogant and you don't think you know everything
- You listen
- You're always in learning mode
- You want to do better
- You know you can be better

If you know me—everything I teach can be applied at work and at home. Think about each of these places when you think about being coachable. Kindness speaks for itself. The only thing I'd add to this second rule is to be kind to everyone. Always. No matter what.

Life Lesson Two: My Kindness Mentor

Okay, so after "Above all else," what is the next take-away? It has to do with being inspired by people around you. I'm going to share one of the best examples I've experienced. I hope you find it just as inspiring.

There are those special people in our lives who, anytime you're around them or talk to them, you *will experience moments of inspiration.* They are just being themselves. My Uncle Charles Douglas Seigrist is such a person for me.

I've written about being named after him before but, as a reminder, I have the honor and privilege of having his middle name. Since my earliest memories, this has always been something I'm extremely proud of. Some might think it's because he had such a successful military career; who wouldn't like to be named after a Lt. Colonel in the U.S. Army? But I got the name way before that milestone in his life.

My Uncle Charles is the youngest of five children. He was raised by his single mother and his youngest sister (my mother). In the odds column of people who will most likely be successful, the numbers for Uncle Charlie would have been pretty low. That's because he grew up in a time when a single mother raising three of her five children would simply not be able to give him some of the benefits afforded to other people.

Charles has often said, "I learned everything I NEEDED to know by the time I finished sixth grade."

Recently, when he and I were visiting, we got to talking about growing up poor. (I'm sure we all have the "We were so poor …" stories.) I shared with him that one year when Melanie and I were first married, we were so broke that on Valentine's Day we both went to the Hallmark store, selected cards for each other, gave them to each other to read, and then put them back on the rack and left the store.

He then shared with me that he had onion and mustard sandwiches growing up. Yikes!

In that conversation, Uncle Charlie shared a nugget from his oldest sister, Louise, that will forever be a quote I'll cherish: "We weren't poor; we just didn't have any money."

> ## "We weren't poor; we just didn't have any money."

Most of you have heard that behind every successful man stands the true image of his strength—his wife. She provides the support that allows him to go out and conquer the world. That person for Charles is our sweet Aunt Carol. She grew up in a military family and knew what was in store for her. They have raised three daughters, who love them and each other dearly.

Uncle Charlie didn't have a good example of a successful marriage, so they just had to learn together along the journey. "Carol and I both simply tried to do what we thought was the right thing … with each other and the children. Made a lot of mistakes along the way, but none were fatal and we were quick learners … my mistakes were honest and part of a learning process."

I love this part: "We are not Charles or Carol. We are Charles and Carol … one word … one entity. Today she is my lifelong friend and companion, and the love of my life. She was and still is the most beautiful female I have ever seen. I am lucky she is as beautiful inside as she is outside."

"Divorce was never in our discussion … murder maybe, but not divorce (just kidding here)!"

His advice on a career: "The single thing that keeps most people from success is opportunity … so take advantage of every opportunity presented or made … and always be the one guy who gave someone else an opportunity."

Since retirement, Charles has enjoyed cooking, reading, spending time with his family, and mentoring his grandchildren. He has also completed four years of study at the University of the South in a program called Education for Ministry, which teaches you how you can develop your own personal ministry in life and your own spirituality.

"Being a grandfather is the best time of life … it carries with it a huge responsibility to live up to all the things you've taught your children. To continue to be the one who sets the standard and be the example."

With such a decorated armed services career and a lifetime of creating value in people, what he said at one of our family reunions has stayed with me now for decades:

"Each of you is going to spend the majority of your life working. At the end of that work life, when this old world has gotten everything out of you that it can—you will be discarded. Thrown away. All you'll have left is family. Make sure you are kind to them along the way!"

So, I urge you to keep your family in first place in your life. In the end, they will be the ones who are there. Be so intentional every day about being kind to them, so much so that when they think of you, "Kindness" is their first thought! That's mine when thinking about my Uncle Charlie.

> "If you can't be kind to your family, nothing else really matters!" - C. D. Seigrist

Life Lesson Three: Give Your Blessings

If you haven't seen the movie *Steve Jobs: The Man in the Machine*, released in 2015, it's pretty painful to watch. First, you have to understand that I am a huge Apple product disciple. I've owned every release of the iPhone since it came out. It's really amazing to me that Steve had such weak leadership skills. Sadly, it was in every area of his life.

There's another movie that portrays the opposite. It's the 1946 movie *It's a Wonderful Life*. That movie came to my mind as I watched *Steve Jobs* and how he dealt with everyone around him. He constantly crushed the spirit of his young daughter, her mother, his team, and all those closest to him in the workplace. Yet in the eyes of the world, he is the icon of success. I've always said that you really learn more from bad bosses than good ones, and Steve Jobs is a perfect example of that.

Jacob Blessing Joseph

From all the way back in the Old Testament days through today, there is nothing more important to those who look up to you than to receive a blessing from you. In those Old Testament days, it was actually a formal ceremony given to the oldest son by his father. The most famous blessing gone bad was when Jacob and his mother, Rebekah, tricked Isaac (whose eyesight was bad) into believing that Jacob was actually Esau, the eldest son. Jacob essentially stole the blessing that belonged to Esau. Jacob (Israel) went on to be the father of the 12 Tribes and gave his blessings to his sons, as depicted below.

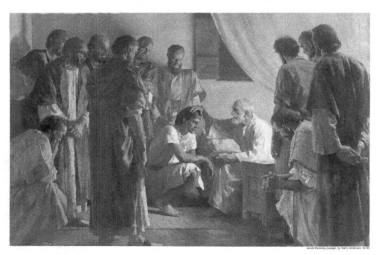

Jacob Blessing Joseph, by Harry Anderson. © IRI

Modern Blessings

In our modern society, we no longer have formal blessing ceremonies. But make no mistake, the longing for the blessing exists nonetheless. I'll always remember when my kids were young and we'd go to the city pools in Weatherford and Altus, Oklahoma. We always drew in a crowd of other kids because I was spending time with my sons, teaching them how to swim, and they just wanted to be near us. Jared and Travis would hit milestones like going underwater, diving off a board for the first time, doing their first flip off the board, or swimming underwater across the entire width of the pool. I was there to cheer them on and let them know how proud I was of them. I can't tell you how many times the other kids gathered would say, "Watch me! Watch me!" They were starving for the attention (blessing) of a parent.

As my kids grew up, the specifics changed, but the results did not. Whether it was playing golf, coaching their Little League team, fishing, camping, snow skiing, church camp, Sunday school, or work, they got their daddy's blessing (teachings) daily. Though my sons are in their 30s and 40s and we are separated by many miles and states, there is not a week that goes by that we aren't in touch with each other. We share victories, struggles, sports scores, and jokes through phone calls, emails, texts, and FaceTime.

Melanie has been the same way with our daughter, Taylor. My wife has built value into Taylor's life every step of the way. Melanie coached her sports teams, taught her life lessons along the way, and shared many special moments throughout the years, giving her encouragement to just be the best *she* can be. "Do not compare yourself with others. Just do the best you can do, and that is good enough."

This is kindness in living color!

Kindness in the Workplace

This commitment to kindness is exactly what is missing in most workplaces today. If you think about how many hours a week you spend on the job, it's probably more waking hours than you spend at home. Workplace relationships are viable on all levels. They work with your inner circle and outer circle. They work with your peers, your direct reports, and your indirect reports.

Whether it's just a "Hello, how was your weekend?" or "How was your child's game?" or even a quick comment about a presentation, sales or margin milestone hit, or a negotiation in a meeting that was off the charts, you're giving out a blessing. I've learned that after you've asked someone to host a call or meeting, they will most likely be waiting after it's over for you to stop by and let them know how they did. *Don't make them ask!* No matter the age or position of those around you, they need your kindness to come through as a blessing.

In the movie *Steve Jobs*, Steve is walking down a hallway before a product launch, and one of his team members comes through the door. The employee is looking at Steve the whole time. As they pass, he says, "Hi, Steve." There is no reply from Jobs. "Woz" (Steve Wozniak), Apple's co-founder along with Steve, begs Steve before every launch to acknowledge the Apple II team from the stage. Woz understood how hard his team had worked to make Apple a successful company and how starved they were for just a brief acknowledgment (blessing) of that hard work. Jobs refuses.

In another scene, Steve actually threatens to expose the failure of programmer Andy Hertzfeld during the launch. They are trying to get the computer to say "Hello." Andy never forgot this. It's the best example of a reverse blessing. Again, this is an example of what NOT to do. My favorite part of the movie was when Jobs's head of marketing, Joanna Hoffman, finally tells him the raw truth about what's important in his life. Per her assessment, it is his daughter. Hoffman tells him to "fix it." She had witnessed 19 years of failure on Jobs's part to be a good father. "What you make isn't supposed to be the best part of you. Being a father, that's what's supposed to be the best part of you," she tells him.

Back to the Family

My wife, Melanie, gives me her blessings all the time. There's no doubt that she is my biggest fan. Meme and Papa, who are my wife's mom and dad, never visit without giving me their blessing. And if you knew Melanie's aunt and uncle, Ken and Sharon Delfeld, you would know that they are blessing-givers. They've been the best example in my life of how to connect with people. If you watch them at any family gathering, they give their full attention to each person there, one-on-one, regardless of age. They spend time with them, hearing their story and giving encouragement. They faithfully send birthday cards to everyone in the family. They illustrate kindness like you can't imagine. And every time I talk to my Uncle Charles Seigrist, he gives me his blessing.

As I have led my teams, I've tried to learn from all these examples. Everyone in the workplace whom you come into contact with will either be better or worse because of your influence. It's your decision. I hope you can use the illustrations in this section to see the good ones and the bad ones and model your lifestyle after the good ones.

Life Lesson Four: What's It Like to Be on the Other Side of Me?

You can't talk about being kind without knowing this one truth that was taught to me by Dr. Randy Ross. Dr.

Ross is a keynote speaker who spoke to us on the topic of feedback as discussed in his bestselling book *Relationomics*. In his speech, he shared what it's like to raise boys, and then what it's like to raise his one daughter. One of his mentors advised him to set aside special times to spend with his daughter throughout her life. So, early on, he had many tea parties with her. As she grew up, he spent many other special times with her, like taking her to the park, going to the movies, and taking trips. It was during these times that he asked her for her feedback on how he was doing as a dad. He asked her if he was a good parent. Many of her comments were positive, but she did give him some constructive feedback as well.

He calls feedback "The Breakfast of Champions" for these reasons:

- It demonstrates humility
- It reveals potential blind spots
- It increases self-awareness
- It helps us see ourselves as others see us
- It slows us down long enough to "smell our own exhaust"
- It provides insights into growth
- It strengthens partnerships

"What's it like to be on the other side of me?" is a question that I've used many times since, when coaching people. I've challenged many of my direct reports that when they are ready to hear the answer, then ask the question. But you'd better be ready to hear what is said. I can guarantee you that if you are kind, you'll always be able to handle the answer to this critical question. Everyone you meet is someone's son, daughter, mother, father, sister, brother, and so on. Treat them the way you'd want your family member treated.

Life Lesson Five: Winning with Kindness

It is my firm belief that if retailers could make "Be Kind" an embedded part of their culture, and truly teach by example what it means to be kind, most customers would be loyal and shop with you, even if they knew they might pay a little more. That's the one element that you do not get online or in most other retailers.

Before COVID-19, the competitive landscape was already changing in the retail world. Customers had more options than ever before due to the explosion of smartphones and eCommerce. These sites had all the items and prices of almost everything we sold. You have ZERO FORGIVENESS today from these customers. Not because they are mean; they just no longer have to settle. Most likely, they will not even say anything. They will silently stand in your store and order online whatever they can't find in your store. Or, they will go online to find the same product at a lesser price. They may even create a pickup order from a competitor and drop by after leaving your store to get it.

So, how can retailers use kindness to win in this difficult environment? By having engaged team members who truly care about the customer experience.

I learned how important being kind to customers was early in my career at United Supermarkets of Oklahoma. The motto of the company was "Home of the Personal Touch." It was a family-owned business, and most of the stores had generations of families who worked for the company.

While there, we were taught to learn our customers' names and call them by their names every time they came in. And not only did we learn their names but their families' names as well. We were in a lot of smaller towns, so most likely, our customers coached our kids, or we coached their kids. We very likely went to the same churches and saw each other in many places outside of our grocery store.

I remember very vividly when our first son, Jared Stephen, was born in Weatherford, Oklahoma. We received an abundance of gifts from my customers. That's how close I was to my customers. I cared for them, and in return, they chose to be involved in my personal life also.

One of the things I've believed for years is that if you shop anywhere and don't leave angry, then that was a good shopping experience. I also know that although most customers may be disappointed because you may be out of something, they are off-the-charts dissatisfied when they encounter a disengaged employee. Or worse, if they run into an employee who is outright rude. With over seven billion smartphones in the world and billions on social media, you'll find out quickly when someone has been mistreated in your store. The in-store experience *must* trump online convenience and price. And the trump card is being kind.

Your Challenge

Since you are now very aware of the blessing, I want to challenge you. Don't let a moment go by this week without giving it freely. Give your blessing to your spouse, your children, your team members, your boss, your friends, your inner circle, and your outer circle. Even to a stranger who might be saying to you in their own way, "Watch me! Watch me!"

As Chief Operation Officer in the supermarket business, I'd travel to visit all of the stores. Store employees usually knew I was in their town after I'd dropped by the first store. The manager of the next store had been given the heads-up and was usually at the front door waiting to greet me. I was intentional as I walked around every store, taking the time in each department to stop, visit a little, and then give some kind of blessing. Sometimes, I could see them watching me as I approached their department, just waiting on me to make eye contact and connect with them. Knowing the truth of this lesson, I made sure to fill their "confidence tank" before I walked away. This is just being kind.

Kindness does not mean that if there was something that needed attention it wasn't mentioned. To acknowledge a shortcoming is an opportunity for growth and learning. But, as one of my old bosses always said, "You gotta catch the balance and make sure that you point out things that look good, as well as things that need to be fixed. If all you ever talk about is the negative, your team (and family) will just give up, thinking, 'It doesn't matter what we do, it's just never good enough.'" Accentuate the positive and give them praise for a job well done! If you had a camera recording their face after you walk away, you'd never pass on an opportunity to give your blessing to someone!

CHAPTER SUMMARY

As we roll into the future, due to the pandemic, political dissent and disagreement, social uprisings, and natural disasters that are impacting almost everyone alive today, there has never been a better time for kindness to rise up and become mainstream again.

I don't think for a minute that everyone in the world will be kind to everyone in every situation. But what I do know is that even though we don't control everyone, we control ourselves. And if we set a good example of kindness, maybe, just maybe, it will impact those around us. I'm reminded of a story I heard many years ago as we end this chapter.

An elderly man was sitting on a dune above the beach, and the tide had brought in a ton of starfish that washed ashore. These starfish were trapped. He noticed a young man going up and down the beach picking up one starfish at a time and throwing them back into the ocean. The older man walked down to the young man and asked him why he was doing that. He noted that there was no way the young man would be able to get them all back into the ocean. There were thousands of them. The young man said, "You're right." He picked another one up and threw it back into the ocean. He turned to the older man and said, "But I can help this one." He then picked up another one and threw it back and said, "and this one … and this one …" We may not be able to get all the unkind people back into the ocean, but we can help this one, and this one, and this one …

Bring It to Life

1. Write down your kindness ranking—in Personal life and Work life.
2. Give yourself a grade on how you think you're doing in each area, and if you're brave, ask those closest to you for a grade.
3. Write down two ways that you can do better, today.

Reader's Bonus

I LOVE this example that I watched a few years ago, put together by Chick-Fil-A—if we could all remember that every life has a story, we'd all be much kinder to those we meet.

You can find all of the bonuses here: abrighterday. life/bonuses

RULE 3: NO SURPRISES

The third rule, "No Surprises," came about early in my career as a way to help my team understand that I can't help fix what I don't know is broken. It is also critical in personal relationships. (My wife says that the only surprises that are okay are trips! Surprise away with any trip you want to take me on!)

"No Surprises" is by far the most quoted rule from my team. It's not unusual to see this on the subject line of an email or the first thing someone says to me when they walk into my office or call me on my cell phone. To put it another way, this rule could be "Communicate, communicate, communicate." In every area of our lives, we would all get along better, solve problems quicker, and make progress faster if we would simply make sure that the people who can actually help know that there is a problem.

As the top leader in any company, we have the connections to get things done and solve problems. I've always said that anyone on our team should be able to call a sister store, vendor, or wholesaler and get the help they need. Unfortunately, it just doesn't work that way in real life. As a matter of process, everyone should try to solve their own challenges. But the severity of the challenge determines the urgency of asking for help.

Also, I have found myself discouraged many times over my career when a member of the team is more than happy to tell my boss about a problem that I could have solved if I had just known about it. But, for some reason, many people just don't understand this. When someone goes "over my head," bad things happen. First, my boss is surprised. That's never good. Then, I'm surprised to find out too late that an issue that was a "fire prevention" issue has become a "firefighting" issue.

As I discussed in Rule 1, raising your hand to let someone know that you need help is a big part of Doing Your Job. This includes asking for help not only when a problem arises, but also when we are not at our best. If there is something going on in your life that could impact your performance, and you're clearly distracted, let your boss know—they care about you and want to help. We need to be better at preventing fires, so that we don't end up fighting fires. Rule 3, "No Surprises," will help to get us there.

Five Life Lessons on
No Surprises—Communicate Better!

If you're going to get better at communication, then you have to spend some time understanding just how to do that. In the following lessons, you'll read examples and stories that will give you a good foundation for improving the way you communicate and to understand prioritizing the how, what, when, and where of doing so.

Life Lesson One: Communication 101

Communication is a two-way process involving the following elements: a sender, a message, a medium, a channel, a receiver, a response, and feedback. However, it is not sufficient to have only these elements. There also must be cooperation and understanding between the two parties involved.

The "Drive-Thru" Communication Method

I mentioned this in Rule 1, but I want to go through this part in more detail here. This is a simple method borrowed from, of all things, how you place your order when you go through a fast food drive-thru window. The things that we can learn from our everyday lives are amazing.

Here are the steps:

- I say the specifics of my order.
- The cashier repeats back what they think I said.
- I either confirm the order or adjust it.

- The cashier repeats the order again with the adjustment.
- Got it!

This is the best way to make sure that what I said is what was heard. It's not complete communication until I have confirmed that the receiver has correctly understood what I said. We could avoid countless problems in our workplaces, our homes, and our relationships if we simply tore a page from Chick-fil-A.

Are We Communicating Better in Our Modern World?

In a world with more communication devices and media than ever before in history, I think our communication skills are lacking. This is not a good thing considering the biggest disruptor in any relationship is poor communication. That's why Rule 3 is so critical.

Surprises pop up all the time in businesses across the country. These surprises are primarily due to so many people being involved in the communication and details that change on a daily basis. It's hard to keep up. In a world of email overload, people are added to the thread as time goes on. Some threads grow to ten emails or more, all of these going to a different set of people. It breaks down communication.

Here's what I have taught for years about email threads. Once there have been three "reply all" messages sent, stop the thread and set up a call with all necessary parties! It's also imperative to send out an agenda prior to that call with any related documents attached, so that people can review them prior to the call. If everyone follows this simple "No Surprises" process, problems will be nearly eliminated. Plus, there is a paper trail in the event that someone plays the "I didn't know" card. You can prove that they should have known, had they just read the email.

Who Needs to Know What?

To become a better communicator, ask yourself the simple question, "Who needs to know?" The best way to understand who needs to know is to ask yourself, "Whom will this information affect?" Here are some options:

- Your Boss
- Your Peer Groups
- Your Team
- The Supplier
- The Customer
- Spouse/Significant other
- Children
- Mother/Father

Also, consider exactly what the purpose of the communication is. Here are some questions to ask yourself before you initiate communication. This will dial in not just who needs to know, but also what information you need or want to convey.

- Do I need help with a decision I need to make?
- Do I just want to let you know and keep you informed?

If the information you have could be explosive to the nature of business or your relationship at home, then by all means handle that with a personal visit or personal phone call. NOT A TEXT! And the worst would be if someone saw it in a post on a social site. If you think it's potentially bad, it probably is. Don't take a chance. Handle it immediately. Good leaders ask great questions, and sometimes your team isn't sure what they need to share with you and what they don't. You are training them on what's important to you, by the questions you ask.

Getting to the Bad Stuff

It makes sense that we try to avoid the "bad stuff" or keep others from seeing it. I notice this when I'm on store visits. The team members are very aware of the areas of the store I'm focused on, and anytime I head in a direction of the store they know is not in good shape, some will try to redirect my path away from that area.

Don't do that. If the baby is ugly, the baby is ugly. We can't fix what's wrong unless we know it's wrong. Again, follow the rule of "No Surprises." Things will never fix themselves. Take these opportunities to coach your team to get ahead of the issue. Dig into the cause, then set up something to prevent the issue from happening again. That's how we all learn together.

A key to success is to always ask yourself, "What's the worst that could happen?" When a team member comes to me for advice, I pose this question to them. I want to know what's at stake. So, I'll ask, "What's the worst that could happen?" And if their answer is any of the following, it changes the game:

- Someone could die
- I could die
- I could lose my job
- I could lose my business
- I could lose my wife
- My children could disown me
- I could go to jail

If any of these thoughts are expressed, I just look at them in silence until they realize the implications of what they've just admitted to and how that violates the "No Surprises" rule. The best way to coach someone in this situation is to take their story, reword it, hypothetically make it about someone they know, and then ask them what advice they'd give to that person. Over the years, I've found that if you just tell someone what they should do, they never own the decision. Let them come to their own understanding and conclusion.

Life Lesson Two: Prevent Fires by Finding the Spark (Root Cause)

The best way to have "No Surprises" is to understand the root cause that created the issue. In the vein of fire prevention versus firefighting, the root cause of a fire would be the spark that started the fire. As we all know, if there is no spark, there can be no fire.

Five whys analysis example / ONLINE FIGURE 1

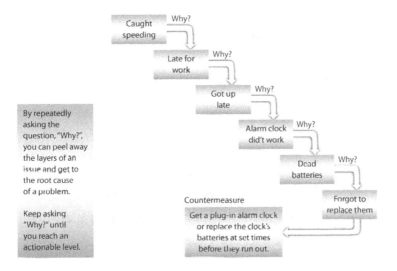

By repeatedly asking the question, "Why?", you can peel away the layers of an issue and get to the root cause of a problem.

Keep asking "Why?" until you reach an actionable level.

Caught speeding — Why?

Late for work — Why?

Got up late — Why?

Alarm clock didn't work — Why?

Dead batteries — Why?

Forgot to replace them

Countermeasure

Get a plug-in alarm clock or replace the clock's batteries at set times before they run out.

Here is an example that happens in just about any retail grocery store on any given day. I've seen it countless times in my 45 years of working in the business.

You come into the store in the morning and have the day planned out.

1. Receive a truck
2. Stock the products from the deliveries
3. Receive all the DSDs (Direct Store Deliveries)
4. Open the store
5. Make sure each department is staffed per the schedule
6. Ensure the cashiers are in place
7. Ensure the customer service counter is staffed

8. Expect all specials and key items to be fully stocked on the shelves by the closing manager the night before

Instead, here is what unfolds in just a few minutes after you get there.

1. The truck is two hours late
2. The DSD receiver called in sick
3. The opening cashier is running late
4. The deli manager had to send one of their team to cover the back door—now they are short-staffed
5. Three registers are down
6. One of the freezers is running hot, and you have to unload everything out of it until the maintenance team can get there
7. The shelves for all your specials are empty
8. Your district manager shows up and is walking the store

Here is how I have learned to handle days like this in the grocery business. It's specific to my experience, but I think it will apply to yours as well. When things don't go as expected, try these steps:

1. Take a deep breath.

2. Pick your priorities; put out one fire at a time, starting with the most critical one.

3. Rally your support managers to help. You're not superman or superwoman.

4. Anticipate people calling in sick. Have some extra help scheduled.

5. Follow up with your closing manager from the previous evening, letting them know the position they've put you in.

6. Let your district manager know that you understand where your hot spots are when they walk in. Let them know what you're doing about it. This lets them know you're on it and you're not surprised by them pointing it out. Don't wait on them to see it and ask about it.

I believe one of the most critical personality traits of a leader is that the crazier things get, the calmer you become. Just like in a family, when Daddy and Momma are calm, the kids will be calm too. If the parents are out of control, it scares the children and solves nothing.

Always get to the root cause and put action items in place to make sure things don't get out of control. Extinguish the spark and you won't be putting out as many fires.

Life Lesson Three: Slowwwww Down

This lesson will minimize the surprises you encounter on any given day. Over and over, when I made store visits, I intentionally walked very slowly. I learned this leadership lesson from Dr. John Maxwell when he shared that his father, who was the sixth president of what is now Ohio Christian University, had the following mantra:

> "Walk slowly through the crowds."

He was a relationship guy who knew how important it was, as he walked around the campus, that he was approachable and got to know his student body and they knew and trusted him. Walking slowly will enable you to establish trust with the team, and you'll also see things you just can't see if you're in too big of a hurry.

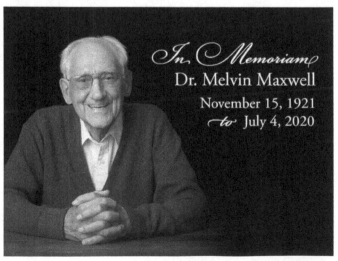

In Memoriam
Dr. Melvin Maxwell
November 15, 1921
to July 4, 2020

When I was a store director, I made several laps around the store during my day. I tried to make sure that the conditions were satisfactory, and that the customers could find what they needed. My mistake was that I walked so fast around the store, I missed many things that needed some attention. I would get frustrated when my district manager came in and saw the things I had missed. How did I miss them? I needed to slowwwww down!

Slowing down means learning to see things that need to be addressed or improved. "Your two eyes aren't enough" is one of my leadership lessons, because as the leader of a store or an organization, there is no way you can "see" everything that needs attention. That's why you must build a team of collaboration and unity. It doesn't matter who sees it; what matters is that it gets taken care of. Think about the average store having around thirty people working in it at any given time. That's sixty eyes. If the team is truly engaged in the purpose of their employment there, they need to be coached to always look at the store the same way you do.

Furthermore, by slowing down, we can learn to have "Customer Vision." That means to look at every area of the store like a customer does.

- Is it clean?
- Are the advertised items fully stocked on the shelves?
- Are the customer service areas staffed properly?

Is the customer looking around? If they are, they probably need help finding something. Go help them! You would never just walk by a mess on the floor. You would either clean it up yourself or ask someone to help you get it cleaned up. Don't just walk by and do nothing. Walk slowly through the crowds and see how much better your vision gets.

Life Lesson Four: Rule Shattered, Now What?

Now, if someone shatters the rule of "No Surprises," how do you respond? What I mean is, if someone doesn't follow the rule and things go sideways, what do you do then? As I'm sure you've discovered, preparing for this contingency is vital to your success and happiness.

This is where communicating the expectations of daily behavior come into play. If you've never had the direct conversation with this person (the rule breaker), you take this opportunity to coach them. The single most important factor in how you handle this is that it must be in *private*. No one should ever be corrected publicly. Never. Neither at work nor at home. Never.

Use the specific details around the situation to help them learn from their mistake. Don't exaggerate and don't understate the facts. Remember, the best way to learn is from a specific situation. Take this opportunity to really drive that home with this person, and I can assure you, they'll use it to help coach their team up as well.

Sometimes you win
sometimes you learn.

John Maxwell

This quote, which is also the title of a book by John Maxwell, is one of my all-time favorites. He even has an edition of this book for teens. I believe this is one of the best answers anyone who's a coach or father can have. Instead of creating drama and making things worse, this should almost always be your response: "So, what did we learn here?" When it comes to "No Surprises," there is always a lesson that can be learned.

I use the following story to advise people to use caution when they think they have learned something, because sometimes a root issue will show itself in a different mask, and at first, you won't recognize it:

You hear a knock at your door and just walk up and open it. Someone puts a pie in your face. So, the next time you hear a knock at the door, you look to see who it is before you open it. You see that it's not the person who threw the pie in your face, so you open the door. Surprise! They put another pie in your face! You then realize that they have a mask on.

Don't be too quick to assume at a glance you know what's about to happen. Keep these two principles in mind when someone breaks the "No Surprises" rule and things take a quick turn south:

- Don't be quick to react
- Respond instead

Responding vs Reacting

Evaluates the situation	Immediate expression
Maintains self-control	Concerned with preservation
Self-regulates	
Long-term outlook	Emotions overwhelm the scenario
Can come to a compromise	Short-term outlook
	Uncooperative
Helps reduce trigger reactions	Can trigger fight or flight feelings

As you lead your team and lead your home life, understand that people will sometimes shatter the "No Surprises" rule. And, regrettably, some may do it over and over. A leadership pillar is to coach them until they get it. Some will get it after one session, and for some it will take multiple sessions. Believe in them and help them get there. It's always more rewarding to help someone conquer a weakness they have than to just discard them. If you value people, make sure you actually value people. Don't give up on them.

Life Lesson Five: The Laws of the Harvest

Growing up in western Oklahoma, I am familiar with the process of harvest—the term we used when it was time to cut wheat. There are some great lessons in farming, and I feel the laws of the harvest offer great guidance on how to conduct ourselves in business—and in life.

Before you can talk about the harvest, you truly must understand the process. And as anyone who has ever been involved in the whole process knows, it's not easy. Sometimes, we create our own "Surprises" because of our unfounded expectations. We have the wrong expectations, and it leads to us getting surprised when we don't need to be.

> "You never plant the wheat today and pull into the field tomorrow to harvest the wheat."

Throughout my career, many people I've worked with simply don't understand that business is the same way. They want to have a meeting to talk about launching a new initiative. The discussion is had and the plan is put in place. Then, within a few days, if the sales don't immediately turn around, they are disappointed. These experiences got me thinking about intent, process, and expectations, and they inspired me to come up with the Laws of the Harvest.

We Reap Only What Has Been Sown

If you want to harvest wheat, you plant wheat seeds. Here are the seeds we "plant" in our business:

- Trust
- Integrity
- Kindness
- Caring
- Focus on our Customers
- Focus on our Team

We Reap in a Different Season Than We Sow

There are four seasons in our annual calendar. In Oklahoma, wheat is normally planted in September and harvested around the first of June. The business connection here is that you need to know the expected "season" that you should expect the harvest to show up. Again, most business initiatives take months or years to produce a good harvest. In today's world of instant gratification, it is difficult for some team members to patiently wait for the harvest.

We Reap in Proportion to What We Sow

If you buy cheap seeds and plant sparingly, don't expect a record harvest. In business, I'm always amazed at the high expectations of better sales, better-performing teams, higher customer engagement, and more efficient checkout results without investing a single dime in systems, training programs, employee incentives, or better equipment to help produce better results.

We Reap the Full Harvest of the Good Only If We Persevere

You will have circumstances beyond your control. You risk the success of your harvest every year. If it's too cold, or too hot, or you have too much rain or not enough rain, it will affect the outcome of your harvest. A devastating hailstorm may hit at just the wrong time and wipe out what was going to be a good harvest. In business, there are so many things beyond our control, yet when bad things happen—and trust me, they will—we still expect to have the harvest we would have had without those bad things happening. What are we thinking?

I'd say nothing affects grocery shoppers more than the weather. If it's pouring down rain, customers just go home after work and don't shop that day. If the roads are torn up in front of the store, don't expect the same sales you had last year when the roads weren't torn up. If you have a new competitor who's opened a store close to you this year, again, don't expect year-over-year sales increases until their honeymoon is over! In this law of reaping the harvest, you have to learn that the "season" could be up to a year before things turn around and you begin to see the numbers that you hoped for before the event happened.

We Can't Do Anything About Last Year's Harvest, but We Can About This Year's

The biggest mistake most people make is not putting last year to bed and focusing on this year. You can't change a single thing that happened last year, but you can change almost anything in the coming year. We had a few harvests in Oklahoma when I was growing up that were just awful, for all the reasons listed above. It was imperative that we put all our focus on the next year's crop and try to do some extra things in the coming year to help offset the loss from this year.

I've experienced bad harvest years in the grocery business as well. The majority of the time, it was due to things happening beyond our control. We have faced things like new competition, hurricanes, supply chain/

trucking disruptions, increasing fuel prices, manufacturing interruptions, and employee challenges due to worldwide health issues. Issues like this have recently played a major role for many businesses, both large and small. This is a life lesson for everything you go through: don't be surprised if some years the harvest yield is not what you hoped for. No farmer would ever tell you they've had ten years in a row of record harvests.

CHAPTER SUMMARY

The key to Rule 3, "No Surprises," is great communication. And great communication comes from understanding the basics of communication. It comes from confirming what you have heard and knowing who needs to know what. You can put out the root cause of the fires you face if you trace it back to the spark that started the fire. Slow down and take your time. You will be a much better communicator if you do. Anticipate that this rule will be broken and use that as an opportunity to improve the process. And don't forget the Laws of the Harvest. They will help you to correctly adjust your expectations.

Now, let's turn to Rule 4, "No Drama." Can you imagine how that will improve your life and success?

Bring It to Life

1. Write down your communication ranking—in Personal life and Work life.
2. Give yourself a grade on how you think you're doing in each area, and if you're brave, ask those closest to you for a grade.
3. Write down two ways that you can do better, today.

Reader's Bonus

The Best Ted Talk I've Seen on Better Communication

When your job hinges on how well you talk to people, you learn a lot about how to have conversations—and that most of us don't converse very well. Celeste Headlee has worked as a radio host for decades, and she knows the ingredients of a great conversation: honesty, brevity, clarity, and a healthy amount of listening. In this insightful talk, she shares ten useful rules for having better conversations. "Go out, talk to people, listen to people," she says. "And, most importantly, be prepared to be amazed."

You can find all of the bonuses here: abrighterday. life/bonuses

Rule 4: No Drama

When I'm speaking to a large audience at regional and annual conferences in the grocery space, this rule is always a crowd favorite because everyone can identify with it.

To begin, let's talk about what drama is and what it is not. This is vital to understand how to apply the rule to your business and family life. Drama *is not* a family member dealing with an illness or the inability to pay their bills. Those are realities of life. We should all be concerned about those kinds of situations and help others as much as possible to get through those valleys. Drama *is* unnecessary fear and anguish brought on by exaggerated facts or feelings. Drama also occurs when we continually talk about these exaggerated facts or feelings. We talk about them to the point of driving those around us nuts.

The "Drama Towel"

The "Drama Towel" is an image that I have found particularly helpful in illustrating how to reduce drama at home and at work. Imagine, if you will, that every time you enter or exit your home, there is a small towel hanging on the wall next to the door. We are going to name this the "Drama Towel." What you do each day when you come home is wipe all your work drama on that towel, enter your home fully dedicated to the people who are in there, and be fully engaged in your role.

Be present—fully present. Trust me, your three-year-old could not care less about your "bad day" or the latest office gossip. They just want you to color with them, watch a movie, or just play with them.

Then, as you leave for work the next morning, stop. Wipe all your home drama on the drama towel and go to work and be fully engaged and present there as well. Then simply apply Rule 1—Do Your Job.

Whether the culture is at work, at home, at school, at church, or any other place you gather with a group of people, everyone there wants to have a healthy culture. We'll discuss more on culture in Rule 5, but make no mistake, eliminating drama will destroy the "ugh" feelings you used to experience when you walked into any of those places or situations. Drama is something that you can actually *feel*. When there is drama in any gathering place, you can feel the coldness and discomfort. Or drama can sometimes cause a general feeling of not being warm and inviting. Who wants to be in that kind of place?

What's the biggest reason you shouldn't bring your work/school drama home? Your spouse, parents, or significant other will want to fix it. But they can't. So, leave it at work. For sure, you should bring home and share the exciting details and accomplishments of your job. Just not the drama. The same goes for work. Your work associates are just that—fellow workers. Although they might have a passing interest in the drama from your home, they want to focus on work. Use the drama towel to keep these parts of your life separated. You will be much better at home and much better at work.

Now, let's dive into the Five Life Lessons about the No Drama Rule. This rule is definitely one that you will want to follow. It makes your life simpler and happier. And everyone around you will appreciate your presence more.

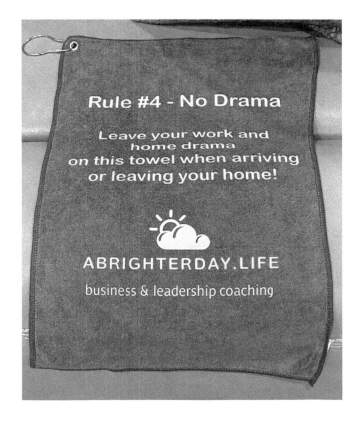

Five Life Lessons on
No Drama—Love Better!

Life Lesson One: The Damage of Gossip

I believe one of the biggest creators of drama is gossip.

Gossip is shared by the misinformed, who often sound like fools, while creating ongoing drama and disorder.

QUOTLING.COM

A few years ago, I attended an Exchange Conference put on by the John Maxwell team. One of the fun things about Exchange is that they take you out on an excursion. And they don't tell you beforehand what the excursion will be about. This conference was in Atlanta, and the excursion began at the Delta Airlines World Headquarters, where Ed Bastian, President at that time, now current CEO, spoke to us about their leadership initiatives. We then boarded a plane with no idea as to where we were going.

About thirty minutes into the flight, we found out we were headed to Nashville to meet Dave Ramsey (the author of *EntreLeadership*, and of the nine-lesson course, "Financial Peace University") at the Country Music Hall of Fame. There he talked about how his company handled office gossip. They didn't. You would be terminated if you were a chronic gossiper. He shared that in the early years of starting his business, he'd have to handle it, but over time, it would just get stopped at the employee level. He shared that it was such a healthy culture that if a new person walked into the break room and started gossiping, a fellow worker just looked at them and said, "Hey, stop. We don't do that here!" Since then, he's not had to terminate a single employee for gossip.

At an early age, I was taught how to handle gossip (or false things said about myself or others) by my Sunday school teacher Willa Belle Hardin. She said, "Your friends don't need an explanation, and your enemies wouldn't believe it anyway."

"Your friends don't need an explanation, and your enemies wouldn't believe it anyway."

I can tell you, 46 years after hearing it for the first time, this is still one of my most quoted statements. I use it when things are in a critical state and a close friend needs to hear it. After hearing the quote, they usually reply, "Thanks, I needed to hear that!"

Willa Belle was a remarkable woman whose wisdom about gossip likely emerged from her experience in the newspaper business and her Christian values of true forgiveness and acceptance of people. She was a retired businesswoman who spent most of her career as the office manager of the *Clinton Daily News* in Clinton, Oklahoma. Because she was involved in the local news, she had access to a lot of facts in the community and a lot of gossip and hearsay. In her personal life, she was also the target of gossip. She raised two children on her own and was one tough lady. Back in those days, a single mother raising children in a small Oklahoma town brought about some criticism in the community. She passed away in 2006, but she will always be one of my life's best encouragers. She definitely made a difference in my life. She loved her family, music, church, and sports. (It was always cool to me to be able to talk sports with my Sunday school teacher, who was a lady.) And I hold an extra amount of respect for her as a single parent trying to play dual roles in raising their family.

If Willa Belle were alive today and could see all the drama that is exposed on Facebook—a drama cesspool in our world (really, all social media platforms are)—she'd probably just copy and paste her wise words in comment boxes throughout any given day. There is so much information out there that's just not true and usually never tells the whole story. I'm always shocked by what people put out into the world. They don't have a common-sense filter, and they are certainly what we call "Keyboard Warriors" who just stir up drama.

In a world of gossipers and those who choose to believe the worst in people, I always have a comment for them.

> "If you won't believe everything you've heard about me, I won't believe everything I've heard about you!"

One characteristic I've tried to have is to make up my own mind about someone based on exactly what I know or have experienced with them. I try very hard to never base my opinion on what I've "heard" about them. How many times, once you've gotten to know someone, have you changed your opinion of them? Maybe you thought, "They are nothing like I'd heard they were."

Throughout my life, I've had an inner circle: friends, family, and co-workers who will stand by me, judgment-free—under any circumstances. They are always there—not once, but every time. They'll defend me to a fault. And they will do it for a lifetime. I thank God for these people in my life. We all need people like this in our lives. We also need people in our inner circle who will call us out and help us along the journey to be the best possible version of ourselves. Spouses are especially good at that … lol.

When it comes to gossip, and the damage it can do, I want to be the friend Willa Belle had in mind when she said, "Your friends don't need an explanation …" And we all need to be like the team in Dave Ramsey's organization: "Hey, stop. We don't do that here!"

Life Lesson Two: Do It Because of Who YOU Are

All of us have encountered drama in our lives. And it will continue throughout our time on earth. This lesson is based on the "Second Greatest Commandment"—love your neighbor as yourself—which I will return to in a moment.

Before that, I'd like to look at how YOU can control your response to harm, or drama, that is directed toward you. Throughout my lifetime, I've seen and experienced drama from some of the most unlikely people. Many times, it wasn't a direct hit, but a hit where I was blindsided. I believe the root of most blindside hits is that the people involved simply don't have all the facts. Without the facts, they jump out there and take a stand on a topic that might involve you and then go public with it. This is such a shame because now you must decide what your response will be. I've found this method to be effective:

1. Ignore it
2. Don't feed it
3. Move on

When I was the Chief Marketing Officer at Sprouts, that's how I advised my team to deal with Facebook posts that just weren't true. Those negative, untrue posts can't be left on the Facebook feed of a business because most people believe everything they see online. My instructions were to delete the post and ban the user. We never took them on; we never tried to give more details or defend ourselves from what they said. I believe this to be good advice to deal with untrue or negative drama. The only time you can't "ban the user" in your life is if it's a family member. Or someone you work with.

I think COVID and the politics around vaccinations probably split more families than anything in modern times. I've heard story after story during the pandemic where, if the whole family didn't agree on the topic, it split them right down the middle—and not gently either. It ripped apart families that you never thought could be torn apart. But it did. And it's happened over and over again.

Well, after several years of battling COVID, there are as many "pros" as there are "cons" for what the results of the vaccinations have done or not done. Honestly, I don't know the real answer here, and quite frankly, nobody ever will. I don't think that's the issue at all anyway.

If you're a believer and believe in your heart that we're all children of God, and you believe what the New Testament teaches as the "Greatest Commandment," then love your neighbor as yourself. Not for them, but for YOU. After all, you can only control YOU. So, forgive the hurt and move on.

Not to get too "preachy" here, but it's easy to love everyone who believes in everything you do and agrees with your political and social beliefs. The real challenge comes into play when you don't agree. We can still get along, can't we?

"Do the right thing because of who YOU are—period!"

"Do the right thing because of who YOU are—period!"

Being committed to doing the right thing is a great life lesson. When you do, you will see the drama in your life decrease. It's never wrong to do the right thing.

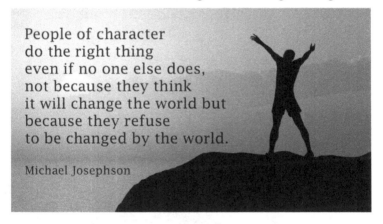

People of character
do the right thing
even if no one else does,
not because they think
it will change the world but
because they refuse
to be changed by the world.

Michael Josephson

Life Lesson Three: Civility, Where Have You Gone?

There are so many toxic cultures in the workplace today that I'm not sure that most people realize that there is something better out there. Drama has entered meeting rooms and it sits at the table right along with everyone else—dropping bombs right and left.

I wish every meeting room had this sign on the door:

Civility includes the behaviors that help preserve the norms for mutual respect in the workplace (or any community). Civility demands that one speak in ways that are respectful, responsible, and restrained. We avoid behavior that is offensive, rude, demeaning, and threatening.

If the lack of civility had a child, its name would be drama. Anytime we feel threatened, we react. Our reactions are different in type and severity. I've worked with many people, and when they feel attacked, they say nothing in the meeting. Instead, they go around to some of their group after the meeting and just stir up drama. They talk not to solve the issue, but to create a diversion of the real issue. This is what I call "the behind-the-scenes character assassination."

In 2017, the incoming freshmen of the U.S. House of Representatives all agreed that civility had left their chambers and they had a desire and commitment to get it back. They declared it the Summer of Civility.

> ### *It's Time for a Summer of Civility*
> *America's political discourse is broken. Too many—whether public servants or members of the public—look upon political adversaries with hostility and vitriol, forgetting that politics is not everything. As former members of the Senate and House, respectively, we prided ourselves on an ability to hold an open and respectful dialogue with people who shared very different views from our own, and we were not alone in that perspective. That has sadly changed.*
>
> ### *It's time for a summer of civility.*
> *We are not under any illusion that these problems can be quickly changed, and we are not naively calling for an end to partisanship. We are, however, challenging all Americans to listen to each other more and to be more open to others' perspectives. Members of Congress are gathering to sign a Commitment to Civility, pledging to act with respect and collegiality toward one another.*
>
> *It is the start of what we at BPC are calling a Summer of Civility—a season for taking the first*

steps toward changing the political discourse for the better. We commend these leaders for stepping up to this challenge, and we encourage all elected officials to make their own commitments. These are symbolic steps, but symbols do matter. Let's do what we can to bring civility and respect back to America's politics.

Recommitting to Civility

The Commitment to Civility Pledge, authored by Representative Mike Johnson (R-LA) in January 2017, was signed by both freshmen Republicans and Democrats. The effort was spearheaded, however, by the Freshman Class Presidents: Reps. Nanette Diaz Barragán (D-CA), Jack Bergman (R-MI), Val Demings (D-FL), and A. Donald McEachin (D-VA).

On Wednesday, June 21, 2017, the Freshman Class Presidents and leadership from the Bipartisan Policy Center recommitted to the Commitment to Civility—a pledge to act with respect and civility—at the U.S. Capitol.[3]

In the years since this was written, civility seems to have left the building once again, but my challenge to everyone, myself included, is to invite civility back into our boardrooms, offices, businesses, and homes.

---

3   *See abrighterday.life/references for this resource*

Life Lesson Four: You Don't Have to Answer the Question

In my earlier years of media training, the marketing team would prepare me for live TV segments. They taught me a simple rule that I still use today in many situations, especially when dealing with drama.

> "Just because a reporter asks you a question, you don't have to answer it!"

They taught me that before I went live for all to see, I needed to have my own talking points and agenda items. And they told me to *always* stick to my script.

I also learned the hard way to be aware of the importance of the things I say. Many times, walking down the hall at work, I would be asked questions and would offer a reply. The next thing I knew was that a new "policy" had been sent down, based only on that quick conversation. As I worked my way up the corporate ladder, there was a point when I was no longer known by my name but by my position. When I was quoted, they didn't use my name but my position. I'll discuss this more in Rule 5—Protect the Brand.

Situations like this are big time drama creators. Learning this lesson can apply to your business life and home life. In my home, when my kids were young, they tried to get away with stuff by approaching us with a clever question to get what they wanted. They would attempt to come to me and get me to approve something they wanted to do. Then, if I nodded "Okay," they would go to their mother and say, "Dad was okay with this. Are you?" We learned pretty quickly to always check with each other before we moved forward. We wanted to make sure we were in agreement.

There's one more application of this lesson I would like to mention. If you don't know the answer to a question or you aren't sure, simply say that. Don't make up something without thinking it through. When you say something that you don't know is right, you're just creating drama. Later, you will have to take back the things that you said that created drama. Take the time to make sure of your answer before you give it.

In many life situations, keep this lesson in mind. You don't *have to* answer the question. When asked a question, it's better to be slow and certain than to be quick and wrong. Never feel the pressure to answer a question if answering that question will create drama.

Life Lesson Five: A Blessed Subtraction

Early in my life, I heard a quote from our pastor, Keith Wiginton, Sr. at the First Baptist Church in Altus, Oklahoma. He simply said that sometimes, when people depart the congregation, they are a "Blessed Subtraction." He was referring to the drama-filled people in a congregation who stir up trouble at every turn. Sometimes less is more. I've always respected the delicate way a pastor has to deal with all the drama that comes their way. It's not like a business where you can just part ways with someone who keeps stirring the pot. In our businesses, we can simply ask them to get off the bus. You can't do that in a church.

With today's focus on mental health, it's the same for those people in our lives who create unhealthy relationships. The sad reality is that sometimes you don't realize how toxic someone is until they aren't there anymore. After they leave, you can feel a calmness in the atmosphere. That is how you know that the person leaving was indeed a "Blessed Subtraction." And it is truly a gift.

Sometimes the No Drama Rule means that you must remove a drama-filled person from your life. Some people don't know any way of life besides drama because that's all they've ever known. Another quote from Pastor Keith was, "It's hard to learn something new if the first time around you learned it wrong." If someone grew up in a drama-filled life, rest assured, they think this is normal and even feel something is missing if there isn't constant drama happening.

We can help to have less drama in our lives by recognizing "drama triggers" in conversations with those in our lives. When those triggers happen, we should immediately steer the conversation in another direction. Sometimes we can't completely remove a toxic relationship from our lives. However, we can limit the time we spend with that person. It could also be as easy as never being alone with them. Having other people around will help keep the conversation from going down the path of drama spewing.

As I mentioned in the introduction, Rule 5 is all about culture. My definition of culture is the emotion you feel when you go to a place or meet with a person. Or, it's the emotion you feel when you leave a place or a meeting. We all need to learn that if we feel "icky" when we walk away from someone, they are toxic and they need to become a blessed subtraction from our life.

Today you can Google "drama-filled relationships" and get all kinds of advice on how to deal with drama addicts. Many of the articles I read said that drama addicts have many of the same traits as people addicted to drugs, alcohol, or other substances. It's the highs and lows of emotional outbursts that feed the drama addict. Like all the others, only drama addicts can fix themselves. You can't. I can't. No one else in their lives can.

To apply the lesson of a "Blessed Subtraction," you first have to identify the drama addicts you encounter in your life. Look for a common denominator when it comes to people on your team or in your family who have a lot of conflicts. If you see the same person in a large majority of the conflicts—there's your common denominator!

My challenge to you is this: "Make sure *you* are not the common denominator!"

Chapter Summary

More than anything else, I think that drama has robbed people of happiness in their relationships. I'm thankful that today we are all openly talking about mental health wellness and learning what steps need to be taken to improve our mental health and well-being.

As a parent, your child's mental health and well-being are often top of mind. When my wife and I ask ourselves, "What do we want for our children?" In one sentence, what do we want? We have always said, "We just want them to be happy!" Happiness is what everybody wants, and it is what we want for the people whom we love. Don't let drama rob you of daily happiness. Instead, enjoy the happiness that comes from being a positive influence in others' lives.

At the end of every day, most people will ask or answer these two questions.

1. What's for dinner?
2. How was your day?

One of my "happiness" coaching lessons is for everyone in a leadership role to determine at their breakfast table that the people they lead will have something good to say at their dinner table when they are asked how their day was. It's critical that they've had a positive day (with no drama) and can't wait to share that!

Every time you open your mouth, you're either spraying life or spraying death with your words. Choose life, every time!

Every time you open your mouth, you're either spraying life or spraying death with your words. Choose life, every time!

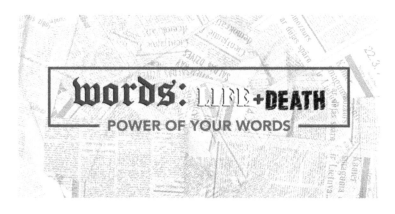

Bring It to Life

1. Write down your drama level ranking—Personal life and Work life.
2. Give yourself a grade on how you think you're doing in each area, and if you're brave, ask those closest to you for a grade.
3. Write down two ways that you can do better, today.

Reader's Bonus

To help you avoid drama at work, as a bonus, I've included this fantastic presentation called "5 Steps to Remove Yourself from Drama at Work" by Anastasia Penright.

You can find all of the bonuses here: abrighterday. life/bonuses

Rule 5: Protect the Brand

I t's time for the final rule. And it's an important one. When I first came up with this rule, I named it "Protect the Mothership," referring to the fact that all businesses must understand that if they don't follow the proper safe handling laws, OSHA laws, and employment laws, they risk taking the mothership down. The rule has evolved since then to focus on something I now consider even more important: the company brand.

Upon going public with Sprouts Farmers Markets, I realized that in everything you do, you represent the brand. This means you represent the brand not only when you are at work, but also when you are at home, shopping, at a restaurant, or at a social event—you *always* represent the brand. I always knew this, but going public makes everything you do in your representation of the brand much worse, if it's bad. Everything you say and do risks tarnishing the brand if it's not professional and appropriate. And you must keep that in mind in all situations and with all people.

The brand isn't the logo or the building. The brand is the thousands of people who work for the company. If you're an executive, you have an obligation to protect their futures by how you conduct yourself. And if you are an executive who represents a public company, keep in mind that you are no longer known by your name, but by your role and the company you represent. Google any executive who has brought shame to a brand, and you'll see what I mean.

My favorite object lesson in protecting the brand comes from a simple red serving plate we have at our home. In 2002, we had a house fire and lost almost everything we owned. We emerged from that event with five boxes of charred, smoke-damaged items that we just couldn't throw away. These boxes were filled with things of high sentimental value we had saved through-out the years.

One of those items was a red serving plate that was a gift from our dear Aunt Fanny. It had been in an antique oak cabinet that had also been in the family for four gen-erations. This plate, smoke-damaged, survived the fire. Every time we see it today, we are reminded of how spe-cial that gift was. It survived a fire that destroyed our home and all its contents. In a way, it represents the heart of our family.

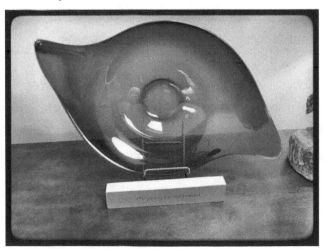

This plate can represent the heart of a company and brand as well. In the same way the cabinet surrounded and protected that plate during the fire, we should all surround and protect our team, our owners, and our families. Whether we are at the water cooler, in the break room, in our work cubes, composing text messages, at the office, or in our homes, we protect the brand.

In our schools, this plate can also stand for the heart of the student body and the learning that should be free to take place there. Be bold to stand up and protect it. Protect the brand in the locker room, in the classroom, in the hallways, and in the dining areas. Protect the brand in everything you say, the way you act, and everything you do.

> "Good choices equal good consequences. Bad choices equal bad consequences."—Bro. Keith Wiginton Sr.

If we always make good choices, we'll most likely harvest good consequences. If we make bad choices, we will most likely harvest bad consequences. (Remember the Laws of the Harvest we talked about in Rule 3?)

Five Life Lessons on Protect the Brand—Only Better!

Life Lesson One: About Your Name

What do you come into this world with? Your name. What do you leave this world with? Your name. What you do between your entry and exit will determine your legacy—your brand. You already have a legacy (brand). Most people think you must be a certain age or even die before you can have a legacy. I believe that as soon as you have influence, you have a legacy. It might be when you become a boss, a parent, or a volunteer.

My full name is Stephen Douglas Black. I was named after Stephen Franklin Vaughn, my great-grandfather on my mother's side. I never met him, although I know he was from Arkansas and had eleven children. My middle name, Douglas, comes from my mom's brother, Charles Douglas Seigrist, one of the most admired people in my life. He has been my inspiration by rising above the way he was raised and going on to be successful in his career. As I shared in Rule 2, he was my "Kindness Mentor."

One of my favorite quotes about being successful despite the cards you're dealt is, "The man/woman at the top of the hill didn't fall there!"

> "The man/woman at the top of the hill didn't fall there!"

Each of my sons shares one of my names: Jared Stephen Black and Travis Douglas Black. I also have two nephews who have my name: Joshua Stephen Roll and Cody Stephen Black. I don't know what it is, but there is a lot of pride in knowing your sons and nephews carry your name. There is also a great responsibility to make sure you don't do anything to tarnish that name.

Whenever I meet someone or get to know them better, I ask about the history of how they got their name. It's a fascinating way to get to know people better. And as many of you know, once I know your middle name and the story behind how you got your name, I will always call you by those two names. (Hey, it's an Oklahoma thing.) I'm sure you've heard of Billy Bob, Joe Bob, Joe Don, and Sherry Bob … Your family name is your brand. How many times have you heard someone make a critical comment about someone and say, "You know, they are from that (fill in the blank) family." Many people have had to learn how to be successful in spite of their family name's reputation.

I recently heard Andy Stanley make a statement. He was quoting his wife. The topic was "What Breaks Your Heart?" They were discussing what we can do to make this world a better place. In answer to this question, she responded, "At the end of my life, I would like people to line up and thank me for …" I asked myself,

"How many people would be in that line to thank me?" Three? Thirty? Three hundred? Maybe three thousand? And what would they be thanking me for? In my case, I hope they would thank me for helping them. I hope I have helped them where they are in that moment, when they needed it, and how they needed it. You've heard of the Golden Rule that we should treat others as we would like to be treated. There's another rule called the Platinum Rule: "Treat others the way they want to be treated." Nothing will bring value to your name more than helping people.

Nothing will bring value to your name more than helping people.

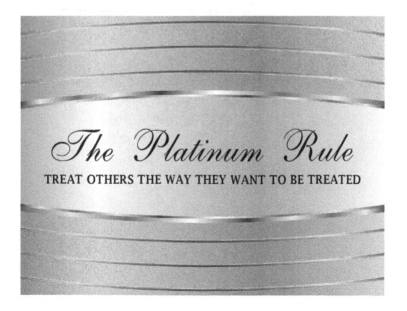

The Platinum Rule

TREAT OTHERS THE WAY THEY WANT TO BE TREATED

Here's how it works. Transformation takes place when people know that you believe in them. You show you believe in them by helping them. Help is more than just money. You can teach, inspire, and coach them. It's always rewarding for me to spend time with my team and teach them something about the business that makes their work life better. I have an even greater sense of success when I help them in their personal life. They are forever grateful for the impact you've had on them.

Life Lesson Two: The 5 Cs of a Difference-Maker

If you were to ask any sports recruiter what they are looking for in a potential recruit, they'd tell you they are

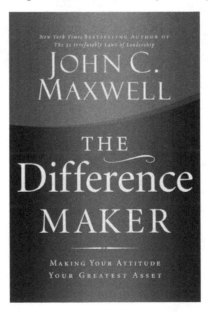

looking for a difference-maker. They are seeking someone who stands out on the team. They want someone who makes the whole team better and ultimately changes the outcome of the game.

The Difference Maker's Creed

I want to make a difference
Doing something that makes a difference
At a time when it makes a difference
With people who make a difference

Over the years, I've known several difference-makers. Some of them have been in business and some in my circle of friends. But most importantly, some in my family. My son Jared Black is a difference-maker, for sure.

Some people light up a room when they walk in. I've noticed that JB lights up an entire city when he arrives. It was while I was thinking about him and the qualities that make him a difference-maker that I came up with the 5 Cs of a difference-maker. Jared embodies these five qualities and it's a perfect leadership lesson for anyone interested in being a difference-maker and giving their own brand credibility.

1. Charismatic

I think of this as "mojo." If you have charisma, you have a personality that draws people to you. It makes people listen to you. It connects you with anyone in your presence. It makes people want to follow you.

2. Curious

A curious person is always asking questions. You see learning as a lifetime quest. You want to know all you can about as many things as you can for as long as you can.

3. Caring

This is when you deeply and truly care about people. It's the core of who you are. You are more interested in the person than what the person can do for you.

4. Comedic

A sense of humor is a vital trait if you are going to make a difference. That trait alone can relax everyone in a room and help them feel a part of the conversation. As the old saying goes, laughter is the best medicine.

5. Of High Character

This is the part of your personality that defines you. It's how you act when nobody is looking. A person of high character sets a bar for themselves that speaks volumes, regardless of those around them. Having high character earns trust, one of the most revered traits necessary to be successful. And honestly, without trust, you have zero leadership value.

If you want to change the outcome of the game, whatever game you're in, then work on making these same qualities a part of who you are. I can guarantee you a better success rate in life if you blend these into who you are.

Life Lesson Three: Rise Up!

There are times in our lives when we simply don't know how we're going to make it through. Sometimes we end up in these situations through the choices we make. Other times, it is through circumstances beyond our control. All of us will end up facing something that we've never faced before.

That is exactly what happened to me four months after I became the CIO (Chief Information Officer) at Sprouts Farmers Market in 2012. I experienced every

CIO's nightmare—a data breach. Those words make me cringe to this day. And if there is ever an event in business that can kill a brand, it's a data breach. This was a very serious business challenge. When it happened, I had no choice but to "Call in the cavalry." Everyone who could possibly help was called in. We had to do things like identify the intrusion, stop it, evaluate what data was stolen, alert our customers via a press release, get a new PCI Compliance certification done, and put new processes in place to ensure it would never happen again. Whew!

Someone from our recovery team reminded me that thieves are always one step ahead of technology. Back in the early days of electronically taking credit cards, the raw data was just a text file on both the POS system and the credit card processing system at the home office. From the beginning of taking credit cards in the '80s, we were partners with a payment company that encrypted all credit card data from the point the card was swiped all the way through to the processor for approval. No credit card data was ever exposed. We were safe. Right? Well, yes, we *were* safe in the '80s, '90s, and 2000s. But in 2012, not so much. The thieves and hackers had gotten smarter.

For the first time in my career, I was having serious conversations with all the major card companies like American Express, Visa, Mastercard, and Discover. I was also having conversations with the Secret Service. Seriously, the Secret Service. Cyber Crime is the single most concerning issue around the world in all retail businesses. It is considered one of the top three issues of all executive teams and boards.

We created a war room with over 20 members from all areas of the business. We worked around the clock for over two weeks. One morning, as I was driving to work, my mind racing with all the details of trying to develop my game plan to conquer this event, two words suddenly came to my mind.

Rise up.

I immediately thought of these two words again. Rise up. They began to swell up something inside of me. I thought of them again. Rise up. I said them out loud. Rise up. I said them out loud again. Rise up. Then I began to shout the words. RISE UP! Again. RISE UP! Again. RISE UP!

That's when I learned the hidden power in these two words. As I entered the office that morning, I had *power*! I had new power. It was a strong and conquering power. I suddenly had the power to destroy this ugly thief who had invaded our lives and threatened to destroy the brand. I found the power to get the knowledge that would allow us to lock out the bad guys. I now had the power to assure our customers that their data was safe with us, and the power to

make sure this never happened again. I possessed the power to give the team the direction and leadership they needed to solve this seemingly insurmountable problem.

The data breach wound up being so minimal that it wasn't even on the radar of the major credit card companies. We don't believe that any data ever got out, and based on feedback from all the companies involved, this was the shortest, most professionally handled breach they'd ever encountered. It was a massive team effort, and everyone involved walked away with major lessons. At the time, we didn't truly realize how minimal it was until the major breaches that came in the years following. Worldwide, in 2014, there were 350 breaches in 11 countries, costing companies an average of $3.79 million in losses.[4]

There are a ton of things we can learn about breaches in this situation. But this lesson isn't about the breach. It is about facing your fears when a giant obstacle comes your way. And it's about being truly committed to protecting the brand.

Since then, whether it's having a tough conversation with a team member, the few moments before giving a speech, finding a solution to a major business challenge, going into a board meeting, or making funeral arrangements for my parents, those two words, "Rise Up," continue to give me power. If today you find yourself facing something that absolutely scares you to death or has you wondering how you're going to conquer it, I encourage you to think these words, say these words—even shout these words:

Rise up, my friend, RISE UP!

---

4   https://www.informationisbeautiful.net/visualizations/worlds-biggest-data-breaches-hacks/

Life Lesson Four: Every Hat You Wear

We all wear many hats throughout our lives. This chapter is about protecting the brand. It's worth spending a little time talking about who you are in each of your roles. I encourage you to take a minute and just write down all the roles you have or have had in your lifetime. You'll be amazed at just how many there are.

Have you ever noticed how many people change hats and become a completely different person? The way they behave depends on the role they are portraying at that moment. I've even seen people who behave like two completely different people while wearing the same hat. (I know you know what I'm talking about. It's normally when their boss is there.)

One of the things I've always tried to do is to be the same person, regardless of who was in the group or audience. Nothing will make you lose others' respect more quickly than treating people differently, depending on who's in the room. Once, I witnessed someone tear apart a team member, and then completely change when the boss walked in. Their tone, attitude, and words suddenly became very professional. Nothing will destroy the culture of a company quicker than having leadership like this. We will cover more on culture in the next Life Lesson, but when you or the people on your leadership team are inconsistent in their treatment of others, the culture is doomed from the beginning.

My son Travis has a leadership lesson named "Hope for Gain or Fear of Loss." It's all about motivating people either by hope or fear. One of the people in my life who's been the best example of being the same person no matter what hat they are wearing is my former pastor, Brother Roy Dobbs, in Clinton, Oklahoma. In the fifty-plus years I've known this man, he's always been the same. Whether he's preaching, attending a family dinner after church, watching a ball game, or enjoying the mountains of Colorado, he's the same guy. Not one time would anyone who didn't know him be shocked that he was a preacher. I've told him many times about how this has impacted me and the high bar that he has set.

This is my Law of the Hats. If you are the same "you" at all times, no matter the role you're playing, you will have more trust and confidence from those who look up to you. This includes your children, your spouse, your team, your peer group, and those who report to you. They will all respect you and follow you. You will have a brand that you'll be proud to call "the real deal."

Life Lesson Five: Your Culture Is Your Brand!

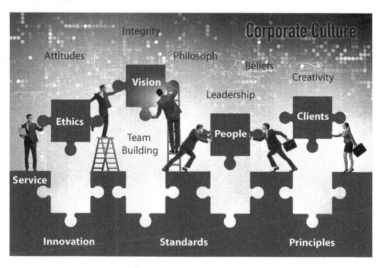

As I mentioned in the introduction to this book, "culture" is something everyone talks about yet can't easily define. Let's break this down a little more. I believe that "Brand Culture" is the emotion you feel when you are going to a store, work, church, doctor, a meeting with someone, or a family gathering. It's also the emotion you feel *after you leave* a store, work, church, doctor, a meeting with someone, or a family gathering.

According to a quotation often attributed to HR Magazine, brand culture is a "unique blend of psychology, ideas, attitudes, and beliefs informing brand behavior, influencing brand experience, and ultimately shaping brand reputation." It is the story of your company and how your team engages with and lives it out in their daily work life. This fits perfectly with the value of the 5 Rules and specifically Rule 5, Protect the Brand.

When speaking to a group on protecting the brand, I always say, "We are the brand." Our brand is not the logo on the building or the words on our business cards. *We* are the brand. Let's break this down into two sections: the personality traits of the brand and the results of the personality traits for the brand.

If your brand were a person, here are the parts of their personality you would evaluate:

1. Their psychology—how do they think and interact with the world around them?
2. Their ideas—are they always searching for new and different ways to approach opportunities?
3. Their attitudes—how positive are they toward people?
4. Their beliefs—what are their core values in approaching their customers, vendors, and workers?

Each of these will inform how a brand is perceived in the marketplace. They will:

1. Inform Brand Behavior—good values will result in good behavior
2. Influence Brand Experience—how people feel when they interact with the brand
3. Shape Brand Reputation—what people say about your brand to other people

Throughout my leadership journey, I've developed this success formula in the retail grocery space to spell out what I think brand culture is:

1. Leadership takes care of the team
2. The team takes care of the customer
3. The customer rewards the shareholder with their business

Your customers' experience will never exceed your team members' engagement level. Or said another way, your team members will never treat your customers better than they are treated by you or any leader in the company. If you have disengaged team members, you have to look in the mirror. Something is wrong and it's your job to find out what that is.

That's why this lesson is all about understanding that *we* are the brand and *we* have to take care of each other. We must make sure that these groups are taken care of by our teams:

- Fellow team members, peer groups, and reporting groups
- Vendors—Most vendors are potential customers, so take care of them
- Online and in-store customers

After years of getting complaints via email, telephone, and social sites, I found that most of the complaints have to do with a team member's attitude. They might show a lack of concern, or lack of urgency to

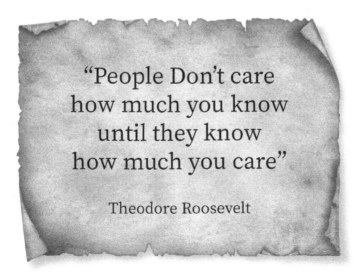

"People Don't care
how much you know
until they know
how much you care"

Theodore Roosevelt

take care of the issue. We've all heard this most of our lives. If we could solve this one thing—caring for our people—we'd solve the majority of the culture problems in our lives.

But I've found that caring for our people is much harder to do than it seems. In its simplest form, when we treat people like we'd like our own family treated, we get pretty darn close. Here's an example that I have used to help people understand what it means to care.

When my sons were old enough, they went to work for the company I was leading. They would come home and share how they were poorly treated. It would make me cringe. I know as a young store director, I made a ton of mistakes in how I treated people. Finally, I accepted this truth: everyone is someone's family member.

Everyone is someone's family member.

If we can keep this fact at the top of our minds when working with others, we will talk to them differently. We will show more compassion when they need help.

> Your culture is your brand. Your culture is your reputation. Protect it. Because without it, you're out of business!

CHAPTER SUMMARY

I've had some people suggest that Rule 5, Protect Your Brand, be put at the top, as Rule 1. But as a leader of thousands of people annually, I think it's a perfect way to end the conversation on the five expected behaviors for everyone inside an organization. A company leader wants everyone on the team to always focus on protecting the brand. That's each one of us, but it's also every product that a customer puts in their shopping cart. We must have the proper food safety handling procedures in place at all times. We must make sure that the thought, "protect the brand," is present in all conversations. There have been many people in the last several years who have lost their job because they didn't protect the brand in the words they chose to say or the opinions they were putting out there recklessly.

In my early media training we were taught, when wearing a mic during a radio or tv interview, to always, always, always assume the mic is hot. That's pretty good advice when it comes to protecting the brand. Always assume you're being recorded. If you're okay with what's being said being sent across the airwaves, then keep talking; otherwise, STOP TALKING!

(I've actually had business cards and pencils with those two words on them and if I was in a meeting and someone needed to stop talking, I just slid the card over to them or waved the pencil in the air to them.)

I will end on a positive note. When I was at Sprouts, I worked with a VP, Mr. Rodney Bonds, who was an excellent communicator. Anytime you were around him, passing him in the hall, or just sitting beside him in a meeting, he would always give you a fist bump. He was just a really cool guy.

When I gave the 5 Rules speech to the executive team at Sprouts, I ended with this challenge, inspired by Mr. Rodney Bonds. Anytime you see each other, give a fist bump and repeat these words in your mind, and even out loud if you want to:

> "Protect the Brand."

Once you hear this challenge, you can't help but think of these words when you give a fist bump. This will always keep the rule at the top of your mind.

Bring It to Life

1. Write down your definition of your Home culture and your Work culture.
2. Give yourself a grade on how you think you're doing in each area, and if you're brave, ask those closest to you for a grade.
3. Write down two ways that you can protect the brand better, today.

Reader's Bonus

To help you learn how to protect the brand, I've included as a reader's bonus a talk by Simon Sinek called "Why Good Leaders Help You Feel Safe."

You can find all of the bonuses here: abrighterday. life/bonuses

CONCLUSION

I hope that as you have read through *The 5 Rules* and the life lessons, you have gained a glimpse into my mind and heart as a leader. I hope that you have been able to see that almost everything that happens in life can become either a leadership lesson, a Sunday school lesson, or a life lesson. I hope that you have the heart to turn everything that happens in your life into a coaching moment. When you are in that mindset, everyone grows and gets better, one simple lesson at a time!

When I started on this journey as an 18-year-old from a small town in Oklahoma, I didn't have a well-mapped strategy with milestones and goals by year or by decade. What I did have was a hunger to learn and a heart for people. Throughout my 45 years, I've learned very valuable lessons about business and how to be successful in the retail grocery space. But the most valuable lessons I've learned were all about people. Early in my career, I leaned into technology and received many certifications. I learned some impressive manipulations with information, and I developed a winning strategy for data and software. But as my career advanced, those certifications had zero value when it came to managing people and understanding how to bring teams together.

If you lead a team of people, I encourage you to do something I've done for many years: provide leadership books (like this one!) to everyone on the team and take the time to discuss the content. In our weekly staff meetings, we would take the first ten minutes of each meeting to review the latest chapter. I placed this discussion as the first agenda item to show that leadership growth was our first priority. I would normally introduce the first chapter, then hand off the remaining chapters for each staff member to lead until we finished the book. It was amazing how each week the lesson in each chapter was exactly what the team needed to hear that week. It was amazing to me how people came to life and shared their chapters in a way that I never expected. Most teams are competitive, and the first time someone on the team put together a PowerPoint with animation and embedded videos, the challenge was on. It became a challenge to outdo the previous week's presentation. As leaders, our main job is to create other leaders, and this is as good as it gets on how to bring the best out in people.

The 5 Rules presented in this book are the foundation of building relationships and culture. They provide a common language of how we ought to treat each other. They can bring more joy to your life than any business success ever will. And as everyone knows, if your foundation is right, everything you build upon it will be strong. Here's a quick recap of the 5 Rules as the foundation of good relationships:

1. I do my job and you do your job
2. I'm kind to you and you are kind to me
3. I don't surprise you and you don't surprise me
4. I don't bring drama to our relationship and neither do you
5. I protect the brand (you) and you protect the brand (me)

With these rules in place, and with everyone in your circles believing in them and committed to them, we will all have brighter days!

What's Next?

I invite you to continue this journey of growth together. And, I have a special offer for the readers of this book. If you go to abrighterday.life/bonuses, you will find a post-

COVID challenge video and a new life lesson I would like to give you. In it, you will receive encouragement and a way to bring all the 5 Rules together.

Submit your comments on the book and you'll be put in a draw to win one of ten free 30-minute coaching sessions with me.

Epilogue: After Your Last Breath

This is my favorite childhood picture. In it are my dad, mom, and my brothers Bobby Gene Jr. and Samuel Lee. I'm the youngest of the three. I've always loved this picture and many times have wondered what life would have been like if the family had stayed together. My parents divorced when I was one year old, probably not too long after this picture was taken. Regardless of the cards that we are dealt in life, we are the ones who control our destiny, and we can rise up and make for brighter days for all those around us.

My Dad

My dad found out on his 76th birthday, April 30, 2013, that he had small-cell lung cancer. The doctors thought they could treat it with relative ease and that he'd have no long-lasting effects of the disease. He hadn't smoked in over thirty years and was still working full-time. Up to that point, he had been healthy and could do anything he wanted to do. He loved to fish, camp, and play golf.

After three months of treatments, and the loss of thirty pounds, we got the news that things didn't look so good. In week four of his last month, we had to move him from the hospital into hospice care. His cancer had quickly advanced, despite aggressive treatment. He struggled just to breathe. One lung had filled up completely with fluid, and the other was about half-full. My wife, Melanie, Dad's sister Betty Terry and her husband, Sam, Betty Lou (Dad's wife), and I took turns around the clock to make sure his last days were comfortable and that he was never alone.

Several family members made the trip to Wichita Falls, Texas, to see him one last time. My sons, Jared and Travis, came to visit and pray for Dad. My cousin, Rick Terry, also came to see him and reminisce about the good ol' days. The first couple of days in hospice were pretty good. Dad loved the vanilla Frosty from Wendy's, and Melanie made the run to get him one on a Tuesday. However, by day four (Thursday) he had slipped into a coma and didn't wake up again.

A couple of days later, on a Saturday morning around noon, an amazing thing happened. His sister had returned to their house to get some sleep, and Betty Lou came to the hospice room to spend the day with Dad. He suddenly moved. I was sitting near the foot of the bed where I could see him. Betty Lou was sitting beside him, holding his hand and talking with me. I thought I saw him close his mouth as if he were going to say something. I didn't say anything until he did it again. It was at that moment I said to Betty Lou, "I think he wants a kiss." She stood up and started lightly kissing him, holding his head, and talking to him. I stood up beside them and at that moment, his breathing slowed, and within just a few moments, he took his last breath.

It was very peaceful but also incredibly impactful.

Moments later, Melanie returned to the room and realized what had taken place. We shared with her what had happened in those final moments. We contacted

Dad's sister, Betty, and her husband, Sam, and we all gathered around him and said our final goodbyes. On August 24, 2013, almost four months to the day from when he found out he had cancer, he was gone.

My Mom

Then, only seven months later, in March of 2014, my mom found out just a few months before her 76th birthday that she had a growth developing in one of her lungs. She had retired from work and was in declining health during this time. We were just a couple of weeks away from moving her into assisted living and had just hired a nurse to stop by every day. The nurse was to make sure she was up, had taken her medications, and was eating.

On September 29, 2014, the first morning the nurse went by to check in with her, she couldn't get Mom to answer the door. She called us at our home in Scottsdale, Arizona, and we talked her through where she could find a key. Sadly, sometime during the night, Mom had gotten out of bed and fallen. She had seriously injured herself and wasn't able to get up. She was breathing, but not doing well.

My wife, Melanie, was already in Oklahoma, moving my stepmother, Betty Lou, to Clinton from Wichita Falls, Texas. So, I hopped on a plane and flew to Oklahoma City to meet my brother Bob and Melanie at the hospital. Mom was fairly alert and doing much better by the time I got there. She knew all of us and could talk in brief answers. But until the swelling went down and further tests could be run, it was too early to know how she was doing. We decided to take shifts at the hospital since she was in the intensive care unit. Ironically, Mom had been in the hospital that same day 58 years earlier, giving birth to my brother Bob, on September 30, 1956.

Wednesday, October 1, 2014, was a day that changed my life forever. As Melanie and I sat with Mom that afternoon, she asked, "Am I dying?" We looked at each other with so many thoughts in our heads. We didn't know how to answer that question. How much information is too much? How much could she handle at that moment? Telling her about her injuries, we said that we hoped not. We assured her that we'd be there to hold her hand if she was. She also talked about her mom and sister that afternoon, both of whom had passed away many years earlier. When we showed her a picture of her brother and asked if she knew who it was, she smiled and said, "my brother."

Charles, whom I shared about in Rule 2, is my mom's baby brother. She helped raise him, and she knew he loved her very much. We also talked about Sam, my brother, who had passed away in 2004. She knew what was about to happen. She told Melanie that she was scared, so we read through the 23rd Psalm together as we held her hands. That comforted her. A calm peace took over at that moment, an acceptance of what she knew was ahead.

Bob came in that evening to take over the night shift. Melanie and I left to go eat some dinner and try to get some sleep. After dinner, we returned to the hotel and were about to head to bed. Bob called and said Mom had taken a turn for the worse and we needed to get there. Mom had signed a DNR but somehow was being kept alive by life support. We knew she didn't want that. The doctor explained to us how bad her situation was and that she wasn't going to get better. His advice to us, which will forever be in our minds, was that if *his* mom were lying there, he would take her off life support. My mom was in constant pain with no relief, even with medication. We decided together to honor her wishes. It was one of the hardest decisions we had ever made.

Once the doctor left, with Bob on one side of the bed, and Melanie and me on the other, we all took hold of Mom's hands. My left hand was on her cheek, and we told her how much we loved her and what a good momma she was to us. Within just a few minutes, she quietly slipped into eternity. At that moment, a tear came out of one of her closed eyes and rolled over my hand. Time stopped and she took her last breath.

Nothing can prepare you for these moments. Nothing.

Now what? For the first time in my life, I didn't have either one of my parents. But what I did have are the things they taught me along life's journey. The hardest days for me since losing my parents are the traditional family gathering holidays, Mother's Day, and Father's Day. And even though I can't contact them on those days, in my heart, we still have a good visit.

The Ultimate Life Lesson

Here is the ultimate life lesson: Bro. Keith Wiginton Sr. always said, "Ten out of ten people die."

So, I ask you, what legacy teachings are you leaving behind for those who remain? What life lessons do you give that are so strong that your loved ones will not only be guided through the valleys, but will also feel your hand on their shoulder, your voice in their ear, and your enthusiasm in their hearts as life goes on?

After your last breath, what will remain? Determine right now that you will leave a positive legacy. Decide that you will choose to get better, not bitter, and always remember, the person at the top of the hill didn't fall there!

It's your move.

No regrets!

AFTERWORD

We adopted our daughter Taylor from South Korea in 1992. Our story has God's hand all over it, and it's like my pastor buddy Zane Newton has said many times:

"You want God to do something so big that the only explanation would be a touch directly from heaven!"

My wife, Melanie, had many dreams about our daughter during the pre-adoption timeframe. Early one morning, she actually woke me up and told me that she dreamed she saw our daughter's eyes open for the first time. In all her previous dreams, she'd seen only a sleeping baby girl. This time, she saw her big dark brown eyes looking right back at her as if saying, "I see you, Mommy!"

Two months later, when we met with the social worker to learn about our new daughter and go over the details of her arrival, we saw this picture and fell in love.

Once we got home from that meeting with the social worker, Melanie went to her journal and looked back through all the pages of her notes. She found the date of that dream when she saw our daughter's eyes open and looking up at her for the first time ...

February 2, 1992 was the date of the dream. February 3, 1992 was the day of Taylor's birth (remember, there is a 15-hour time difference between Oklahoma and South Korea!).

We believe beyond a shadow of a doubt that at the moment God breathed the earthly breath of life into Taylor, he gifted her new mother with that dream. It's a dream that will forever be etched in our minds and hearts.

What a gift Taylor has been to our entire family. It is still amazing to think that halfway around the world in South Korea, a little girl needed a family to love her and in a small town in Oklahoma, USA, a family needed a little girl to love and complete their family. Miraculously, God brought us together!

Brother Zane was right, "There is only one explanation for this!"

We have decided that a percentage of all the book sales of *The 5 Rules* will go toward an annual donation to Dillion International in Tulsa, Oklahoma, the agency that helped us to adopt Taylor. This donation will go to help other families with the expense of their adoption.

I want to encourage you to read the entire story, and perhaps donate to this fine organization: www.abrighter-day.life/taylor

ABOUT THE AUTHOR

Author Steve Black has over 45 years of experience in the conventional and natural/organic space of retail grocery. His career includes working at Rouses Markets, Lucky's Farmers Markets, Sprouts Farmers Markets, Sunflower Farmers Markets, Bruno's Supermarkets, Buy for Less Markets, and United Supermarkets of Oklahoma. His hands-on experience in all areas of running a business has proven valuable with each role. A leadership-focused student and coach, his passions are growing personally and growing with his teams.

He is the founder and CEO of A Brighter Day (abrighterday.life), a business and leadership coaching firm based in Colorado. He is actively involved with the National Grocers Association and the Retailer Owned Food Distributors and Associates, among others.

He and his wife, Melanie, along with their daughter, Taylor, live in Colorado and enjoy spending time outdoors on their four-wheelers, trout fishing, practicing photography, and traveling to see their two sons, daughters-in-law, and six grandchildren.

ABOUT THE BOOK

What if you could simplify your leadership and life down to five simple rules?

In the book *The 5 Rules,* author Steve Black does just that. Based on over 45 years of leading thousands of employees, he boils it down to only the essential principles that produce results.

For Leaders

Eighty-three percent of organizations say they want to develop leaders. But only 5 percent of them have a plan in place. Culture transformation is not some complex, unattainable goal. It starts with a doable plan that can be repeated throughout your organization.

For Your Family

These same five rules can transform your family. Steve and his wife have used them for decades to strengthen the family bond and to develop strong, generational leadership.

For Yourself

If you are looking for personal transformation, look no further than *The 5 Rules*. Adopt them into your daily life and revolutionize your relationships and your state of mind.

If you are looking for rock solid advice on transforming any culture, *The 5 Rules* is the place to start!

A free ebook edition is available with the purchase of this book.

To claim your free ebook edition:

1. Visit MorganJamesBOGO.com
2. Sign your name CLEARLY in the space
3. Complete the form and submit a photo of the entire copyright page
4. You or your friend can download the ebook to your preferred device

Print & Digital Together Forever.

Snap a photo

Free ebook

Read anywhere